Martin Luther

Mike Fearon

D0042627

Martin Luther
Mike Fearon

Library of Congress Catalog Card Number 92–75600

ISBN 1–55661–306–7

Originally published in English by Marshall Morgan & Scott Ltd. (now part of HarperCollins Publishers, Ltd.) under the title *Martin Luther*.

Published by Bethany House Publishers
A Ministry of Bethany Fellowship, Inc.
6820 Auto Club Road, Minneapolis, Minnesota 55438

Printed in the United States of America

To
my mother and father

Contents

1

The Frightened Boy

Casting frightened glances into the shadows behind him, the boy continued running. His fear increased as the darkness grew all around him. It seemed to him that every shadow cast by the tall trees in the twilight hid a black figure waiting to spring out and grab him. Tears splashed down his face as he rounded the final bend in the path and saw the welcoming lights of home. Shaking and trembling, he ran indoors and threw himself into his mother's arms.

"Martin! What in the world is the matter?"

"The witch!" gasped Martin, fighting for his breath. "The witch! She was chasing me up the path!"

"There, there," comforted his mother, hugging him tightly to her breast. "It's all right now. You're safely home. She won't get you here."

"I was frightened, Mother . . . frightened . . ."

"Don't let your father know you're frightened," warned his mother. "You know you're not to go upsetting him, or it'll be the cane again . . ."

Martin squirmed. Often his father had made him take down the long, thick cane hanging on the wall where it served as a grim reminder. Then Martin would have to hold out his hand—or bend over a chair—to be thrashed by his father, often until the blood came.

"You'd better get into bed before he comes home," cautioned Mother, drying his eyes with the hem of her skirt. She picked him up and carried him through into the bedroom he shared with his younger brothers and sisters. They were all asleep, or at least pretending to be so. Even Mother could be a strict and stern disciplinarian if she thought the children were disobeying her instruction to go straight to sleep.

Quickly she stripped off Martin's clothing, and pulled the nightgown down over his head. She stood over him in the lantern light to make sure that he said his prayers, praying especially for his parents. Then she swept him up into bed and tucked him in. "Go straight to sleep, now. If I hear any noise, I'll be in here to you—and you know what will happen then!"

She turned and walked away, taking the lantern with her. As she reached the door, she turned and smiled at her son. Love and discipline were bound close together in Martin's mother's attitude to her children. She went out of the room and closed the door behind her. The moment she was gone, Martin's terror returned.

It seemed to Martin as though the room had suddenly been filled with black pitch, so thick and impenetrable was the darkness. But as his eyes began to adjust, the pale moonlight from the window allowed him to vaguely make out the outline of the wardrobe, cloaked in deep shadow. But something seemed to move within the shadow. A hobgoblin waiting to spring out at him! Oh, thought Martin, if only he'd gone straight to sleep as his mother had said. Now she would come in the next morning to find his bed empty and himself carried off by the hobgoblin to its home in the dark wood!

The seven-year-old boy turned over and buried his face in the pillow. He tried to think of some happy event in his life that would take his mind away from the dangers of the night.

He could remember that his parents had once taught him that he had been born on November 10, 1483, in a town called Eisleben. They said he'd been christened the next day, and named Martin because that happened to be Saint Martin's day. It was considered lucky to name a child after the saint on whose day he had been christened.

He didn't really know where Eisleben was, but he'd been taught the name and remembered it parrot-fashion. He was afraid that he might be punished if he asked his father where it was. It must be an enormous city, thought Martin, because Father had said that four or five thousand people lived there. He simply couldn't imagine all those people.

The family had moved when he was a few months old, to the little mining town in which they now lived. Mansfeld it was called, and Father said that it was the center of the copper industry. But, try as he might, Martin couldn't think of anything nice that had happened to him since they had been there.

At last Martin thought of something that made him feel more cheerful. The beautiful countryside, of course! Mansfeld was surrounded by lovely valleys, hills, and woods full of wildlife. Its meadows were full of strange plant life. Martin loved the velvety feel of the moss, and loved to help his mother pick mushrooms.

Overlooking the town, on top of a lofty cliff, stood the ancient and beautiful castle of the counts of Mansfeld. Father said that the castle belonged to the feudal lords of the area and that, if Martin was naughty, the Count would come and take him to the castle, to lock him up in a dungeon!

Apparently the Count of Mansfeld, to whom his father always doffed his cap, had built something called a "smelting furnace." The Count was going to let Father operate the furnace. Father would have to hire some skilled workmen to help him, and it would mean that he wouldn't be going down the mines any more. There was some talk that the family would soon be one of the wealthiest in the area.

In spite of the assurances that they were "going up in the world," Mother always told Martin not to think more highly of himself than he ought to think. She had a little rhyme that she used to say:

If folk don't like you and me,
The fault with us is likely to be.

Martin thought his mother must be very clever, because she knew so many wise sayings. "A thief's helper is as bad as the thief," she would say. "A penny saved is a penny earned," "Haste makes waste," and "A good start is half the battle."

Mother was very musical too. She used to sing in order to while away the hours when she was working in their home. Her songs were always simple and direct, homespun and easily understood. She gave him an appreciation for good music, and Martin, through singing along with her, was becoming a good singer in his own right.

Unfortunately, Martin had picked up something else from his parents, something much less beneficial. They were deeply superstitious. Part peasant and part town-dwellers, just as hard work and thrift formed the foundations of their lifestyle, so religious faith and a vivid imagination conspired to fill their heads with ideas of strange, fanciful creatures that they supposed inhabited the world. Martin pulled the bedclothes farther over his head at the thought.

Though they attended church regularly, the God they worshiped—and of whom the priests taught— was an angry, vengeful God. Though it would take Martin many years to realize it, the whole family was being duped. They were being sold a very old-fashioned view of a God who "showered his wrath on sinful man." Any references in the Bible to God as a God of love were generally suppressed, and seldom referred to by the local priests. The people were not encouraged to read the Bible themselves; in fact the book was in a foreign language, Latin, to prevent the common people from probing its mysteries for themselves.

The family was faithful in its worship, and Martin would sit in church every Sunday and gaze in wonder at the priest standing before the high altar. He seemed like an avenging angel who could intercede with God, or bring down judgment.

Martin would sit and listen to the beautiful music—the plainsong as it was called—sung by a hearty choir. He would sit, frightened to make a sound, as his parents went forward with the other villagers during high mass. The priest would utter strange words that sounded to Martin like magical incantations. The whole service was conducted in Latin.

Gradually, Martin had picked up a smattering of Latin words from school. There was a moment when the priest said something that he thought meant, "This is the body of Christ," and he would shut his eyes tightly, afraid to look at what the priest was holding. It seemed that, like a clever conjuror, the priest had somehow turned a piece of bread into Christ's body! Whatever did it look like? Quaking in fear, Martin would sit with his mouth gaping as his parents reached the front of the church and were apparently made to swallow it! What did it taste like? What would it do to them?

Martin wondered how he could escape the watching eye of this God whom, he believed, had sacrificed His own son and sent pieces of the body through time and space to reappear, magically, in the priest's hands every Sunday morning. If God would do that to His own son, what would He do to poor little Martin, who was so wicked that his parents were constantly beating him?

Outside afterwards, the square would echo with the peals of church bells. Martin would brush against the white cassocks of the Cistercian monks, the blacks of the Dominicans and the browns of the Augustinians. These seemed to Martin to be sensible people who shut themselves away to avoid the risk of doing too much wickedness. That seemed a good way of avoiding God's punishment, thought Martin as he turned onto his side in bed.

Before taking the family home for Sunday lunch,

Father would sometimes talk to some of the farmers whose land bordered the farm. They were always complaining about all the holy days that they had to observe. Martin had overheard some of them say that all their religious observations cut down the amount of time they had to tend their fields and take care of their animals.

The farmers had to do what the priest said, because it seemed that the church owned most of the farmland in the area. Even those who owned their own land were frightened to disobey the church in case, they said, they were "excommunicated." Martin was sure that meant that demons with pitchforks would come for them in the night, and carry them down to hell.

In fact, Martin was a bit worried that even if the vampires, witches, and goblins decided not to gang up on him that night, he still had those soul-hungry demons with which to contend. He lay, feeling tense, but now he was exhausted too—exhausted from dwelling on all the perils and evils that he was convinced surrounded him each night.

Turning over, the unhappy boy began sobbing softly to himself. Why had he ever been born? Was there no way he could be sure of being safe? How could he ever be good in God's eyes? Pondering on all these things, Martin Luther—the child who would be Father of the Reformation—softly cried himself to sleep.

2

The Frightened Youth

L uther! Have you learned your lesson yet? Come here and recite the Latin declension I instructed you to memorize."

"But sir . . ."

"Come here at once boy! Have you or have you not done your work?"

"Sir, I . . ."

"Let me hear you recite the declensions of the Latin verb *to conquer*."

Gritting his teeth, Martin did his best to do as he was told, but the expression on his teacher's face told him that he was getting it all wrong. He was hardly surprised when he was told to bend over and touch his toes.

"But sir, you never . . ."

It was no use. His teacher had taken his cane and the swishing noise it made as it whooshed through the air drowned out Martin's words. The beating over, Martin slowly shuffled back to his seat. So much pain, and all for nothing. Why hadn't his

17

teacher been prepared to listen? Martin had never even been given that declension to learn!

It was early in 1498, and Martin was now fourteen years old. As far as he could remember, all his school life had been like this: a hard struggle to learn by rote what was put before him, and woe betide him if he forgot any of his lessons.

Martin remembered when he had first started school, at five years old. Most boys did not start till they were seven, but Martin's father had wanted him to have a head start on the other lads of his age. So, two years younger than anyone else in his class, he had plodded along the lane every day to the village school.

In the tiny village schoolroom, he had been taught alongside the other village boys of all ages. There had only been the one teacher, who taught the whole class from five-year-olds to those preparing for university entrance, in one room, all day, almost every day. Sunday was the only regular holiday and, though there were many other holy days which meant holidays from school, none of the breaks lasted longer than a few days. There were no long summer vacations.

To Martin, there had seemed nothing strange about learning the alphabet as a tiny lad, sitting alongside a burly adolescent studying Latin conjugations.

Latin! What a difficult language that had seemed when Martin's turn had come round to grapple with its complexities. But it was essential if he were ever going to make anything of his life. To be successful, it had been drummed into him, he had to be knowledgeable and well-read. Since all the books were written in Latin, Martin's first task had to be an assault on mastering the language. There had been consolations though. Besides reading, writing, and Latin, the other subject on the curriculum was singing. Not only was singing a great pleasure in itself, it had meant that, when his father had sent him the year before to his new school in Magdeburg, he was able to eke out his allowance by singing in the church choir-stalls. Magdeburg was the seat of an archbishop and the site of a great cathedral with forty altars and a rich store of sacred "relics."

Here, Martin was taught by a brotherhood of pious clergymen and laymen who both practiced a godly life themselves and served others through teaching, preaching, and social service. Martin thought that this was a fine thing. These men, who called themselves Brothers of the Common Life, were not like the cruel and tyrannical schoolmaster he'd known at Mansfeld, and the school was not a "devourer and destroyer of souls," as he was later to describe his old school. Here he was punished only occasionally, and usually with good cause.

"Martin Luther! I shall beat you again if you persist in your daydreaming!" said the loud voice, suddenly, from the front of the class. Martin, in thinking how hard his childhood had been, was absentmindedly looking out of the window.

"I'm sorry, sir," he whispered, and turned his attention once again to his studies. What a fortunate place to be, thought Martin. Why, in Mansfeld, he had once been beaten on fifteen separate occasions within one morning, for trifling causes. As he'd grown older the frequency of beatings diminished, but he had to pay a fine instead every time he misbehaved. As he had no money of his own he had to beg it from his parents, so he often got a beating at home instead!

It was now late afternoon, and school was soon over. Martin left with his friend Johann Reinecke, the son of a neighbor, who had accompanied him on his journey to Magdeburg.

As Martin and Johann wandered down Broad Street, chatting together, they became aware of some commotion in the distance. Running up to see what was happening, the two lads saw a small, fragile man bent nearly double beneath what appeared to be a heavy sack of bread. Why yes, those were definitely loaves that Martin could see peeping out of the top of the sack.

"Who can this be?" he wondered aloud to Johann, as the pale, barefoot man stumbled past.

"Someone said that this man is a prince," Johann replied, clearly disbelieving what he thought he had heard. But one of the city folk confirmed it, as the poor man—who looked like a skeleton, nothing but skin and bones—staggered off up the road.

"Aye, that's Prince William," said the passerby. "His brother is the Bishop of Merseburg, and he's begged that sack of bread for the monks in his cloister. He's a pious, spiritual man who's fasted and chastised himself for many years."

Was this, then, the way Martin would look if eventually he demeaned and denied himself sufficiently to be acceptable to God? Would God love him if he turned himself into a walking skeleton like this man? Martin shuddered. No, he didn't believe that even that would make him good in God's sight. He was too wicked for God ever to love him, he thought. Martin never forgot the sight of that devoted Christian man, emaciated and bent beneath his load, striving to please the God whom Martin felt he could never grow to know and love.

If only God were like the man whom Martin remembered meeting while he and his friends were carol-singing a few weeks earlier. They had sung three verses of their carol outside a door in the city, when a loud gruff voice had called out from inside, "Where are you, you young ruffians?" As the stout oak door began to open, they scattered in all directions into the night, expecting some ogre of a man to burst out into the street and set upon them for daring to beg at his door.

They had returned, shamefaced, when it became clear that the owner of the voice was kindly offering them some sausages! His voice of anger was a mask for his kindness. If only God were really kind behind his fearful appearance! But, for young Martin Luther, that was simply too much for which to hope.

Soon Easter came around and it was time for him to return to Mansfeld to see his family. Walking along the dusty roads with his friend, Johann, Martin saw the leaves forming afresh on barren trees, the bustle of sparrows in the hedgerows, and the whole countryside coming alive again now that the snow of winter had vanished.

The world seemed fresh and newly-made. It was not just the countryside that was changing with the seasons, but the world of knowledge and human affairs. Martin had heard it said that a man named Columbus had recently sailed off into the West and arrived at India—which everyone knew was in the East. Why, that would have to mean that the world was round, rather than flat as people had thought for centuries.

Education, too, was changing. His teachers in Magdeburg seemed intent on making their pupils love knowledge for its own sake. They wanted their pupils to be inspired to learn, rather than be intimidated into learning by the threat of the birch.

Yes, Magdeburg was a place that Martin would long remember as a place of sunshine and the laughter of shared companionship. He would remember it too, as the first place where spiritual devotions had been a part of the lives of those around him. Martin had seen at close quarters the careful observation of private devotions and liturgical practices, for the Brothers of the Common Life kept the round of monastic religious observations. They were intent on spiritual growth, and regarded their regular reading of the Bible as an essential prerequisite for such growth.

As Martin arrived home in Mansfeld, he could hardly wait to get back to Magdeburg after the brief holiday. But his father had other ideas. Martin would not be returning. He was to be sent instead to a school in Eisenach, a town in the opposite direction from Magdeburg.

Martin was shattered. He was going through the changes of adolescence, growing from a boy into a man. Soon his voice would no longer be a boyish squeak, but a manly baritone. At a time like this, he would have preferred to be in a familiar, stable environment rather than attending three different schools within the space of a year.

On his first evening back, his parents seemed pleased to see him. They sat with him beside the fire, and his father told him of his own life, and how they had come to live in Mansfeld. His father, Hans, was the eldest son of a hard-working peasant family, living in Möhra, a fairy tale town of towers and gables set in the heart of the Thuringian forest. As it was customary in Germany at that time for the youngest son—not the eldest—to inherit all the family property, it had become clear as Hans grew up that he would have to seek a better living elsewhere.

Martin sat on the edge of his seat as his father explained how he came to marry Margrethe—Martin's mother—and moved to Eisleben, where Martin was born, in an effort to pull himself up in the world.

It had been a cloudy evening in November when Margrethe had given birth to Martin. His father had been hard at work in the front room, mending his leather apron from the mine, while a neighbor helped with the childbirth. Martin's birth had been an unexpected delight since, a year earlier, the couple's first child had died. Next morning, Hans Luther had wrapped Martin, a few hours old, in an old blanket and trundled through the frosty streets to church for the christening.

Now Martin was to return to the town of Eisenach, amidst the firs and pines of the Thuringian Forest, close to Möhra, his father's home town. Father was optimistic that his kinsfolk would look kindly upon his eldest son and give him food and lodgings. If not, his mother had many cousins in the area who could look after him. But despite the knowledge that he would be surrounded by his kin, Martin faced this new stage in his life with apprehension and fear.

3

The Frightened Student

At Eisenach, Martin lived at first with relatives. Indeed, his parents had so many kindred in the town that they were spoiled for choice. But it seems that either the relatives rebuffed him, or that Martin just could not get along with his parents' kin. In any event, he was soon looking for alternative accommodations.

Martin's new school was the Latin school at St. George's Church. The headmaster was a man named Johann Trebonius, who always opened his classes by addressing his students as "sirs." Martin had never been called "sir" before. He thought that the word could only be applied to his elders and betters—people like his father, whom he would never dare to call "Dad" or "Papa."

One day, Martin was singing for his supper—literally—on the city streets. He had just begun to make up his own songs to sing at the doors of the well-to-do in return for food. The first few times the people had been generous, but gradually they had tired of his singing. Instead of food, he received angry words.

Legend has it that, that evening, when he was hungry and his songs had been scorned at every door, Martin sat in deep despair beside a pleasant cottage. There, under the shade of some fine trees, he sang a very personal song, expressing the grief he felt in his soul.

He was overheard by the good wife in the cottage, whose name was Louisa Cotta. She took pity on the hungry Martin. She gave him all the bread and honey she could spare, and goat's milk to drink.

Louisa listened with sympathy as Martin explained how he wanted to do well at school, but could not get enough food to live. His father had been generous in paying his school fees, and in giving him a small allowance. But it was not enough to meet all his needs.

"Come back to my door whenever you're in need of a meal," said the kind woman.

Martin quickly became a regular visitor. He would talk with Louisa and her husband Conrad, and enjoy their hospitality. The couple soon came to love Martin, who was grateful for everything they did to make his life easier.

Martin was now a tall, sturdy lad, not exactly handsome, but with a pleasant, honest face and lively dark eyes. Though he could sometimes be rude, defiant, and disobedient, he was also thoughtful and sensitive, with the great strength and obstinacy that he inherited from his father.

The small allowance he received from his father was eked out, not only with the "crumb money" he gained by singing from door to door, but with a small amount that he earned from singing in church.

Conrad Cotta's sister, Ursula Schalbe, heard him singing in church and came to know and like Martin through her brother. Ursula took Martin into her home and gave him his board in return for taking her little son to school, and helping him with his homework.

The teenage Luther, with amenable disposition, sat alongside the little boy in that Christian home, coaching him and teaching him his homework. Ursula and her husband were wealthy folk, and it was at their home that Martin first acquired his appreciation for some of the finer aesthetic pleasures in life— music, painting, and tapestry work.

Groups of musicians would often gather informally at the house for private recitals and concerts. It was at these performances that Martin learned the theory of music—of counterpoint, harmony, and composition. It was in that house too, when Martin was at a very impressionable age, that he came into contact with a devout circle of Christian friends. Many priests and laity regularly visited the house, and Martin was profoundly impressed by their deep piety and simple godliness. He was also introduced to men of brilliant wit and cultured conversation, for he was allowed to sit with his elders while they ate and talked together.

Many of the visitors at Martin's lodgings were from the Franciscan monastery, which lay at the foot of the Wartburg Castle, just outside the town. Martin would cherish for the rest of his life those relationships he formed with the abbot and monks.

Foremost in his mind, however, was his schoolwork, and Martin threw himself into his tasks with tireless energy. He mastered the complexities of Latin grammar so well that he was chosen by his head-master, Trebonius, to deliver a speech in Latin wel-coming Professor Jodicus Trutvetter of the University of Erfurt on a visit to St. George's school.

"Keep an eye on that Luther," the professor said to Trebonius. "He'll go far. You ought to prepare him for university, and send him to us at Erfurt."

Such a recommendation came as a great surprise to Martin, who had never been very good at Latin at his first school in Mansfeld. The Latin examination there was "like a trial for murder" he'd once said. Clearly the enlightened educational theories of Tre-bonius were helping Martin's knowledge to increase by leaps and bounds.

After three years at Eisenach, Martin's father agreed to do as the professor had suggested—to send Martin to Erfurt University. With a degree in law, his father thought, Martin would bring esteem to the fam-ily, and the money he earned would enable him to take care of his parents in their old age. Hans Luther was astute about where his own advantages lay.

Hans had even spoken to the Count of Mansfeld about a place for his son as a legal advisor. The right marriage was another important consideration, and Hans had picked out a girl from an extremely rich local family to be Martin's future bride.

Erfurt seemed an enormous city to Martin. Its population of 30,000 was nearly ten times that of Ei-senach. It was a walled city of fine buildings set in the midst of fertile hills. It boasted twenty-three churches, and twenty cloisters for a profusion of different religious orders. The Franciscans were there, as were the Dominicans and the Augustinians. In fact, there were so many monks and priests in the city that it was nicknamed "Little Rome," in homage to the home of the Catholic church.

In this "nest of priests," as he later referred to the town, Martin found accommodation at the student hostel of St. George, which had acquired the name "the beer bag." Discipline was strict at the university and he was expected to wear a gown for all his lectures. When his tutor remarked that disorderly and lazy students were sometimes flogged in the common room, before their assembled fellow students, Martin heeded the warning.

Early on in his student days, he passed through an initiation ceremony in which he was dressed to represent a pig, and then roughly divested of the costume, to symbolize that he was leaving his brutish and ignorant past.

Students had to be in bed by eight o'clock every evening, and to rise at four A.M. (six A.M. in winter). In readiness for the day's lectures, which began two hours later, the students had to formally debate among themselves. Martin became so good at debating that he became known as "the philosopher."

The enthusiasm and industry in study that had marked Martin's days at Eisenach also characterized his study at Erfurt. In the first year, Martin studied the *trivium*, as it was called, of grammar, logic, and rhetoric. In his spare time, he began learning to play the lute.

Martin's academic work was, however, undistinguished at that point in his life, and he was placed thirtieth in a class of fifty-seven. Still, that was high enough for him to be awarded his bachelor's degree.

In the midst of his studies, a deeper importance began to attach itself to everything that he did. In the university library one day, Martin came across a copy of the Bible and, for the first time, began to read it for himself. For as long as he could remember, he had heard the Bible read aloud in church on Sundays, and during meals at college on weekdays. Martin was startled to find that the passages with which he was familiar constituted a very small fraction of the whole book. There were hundreds of thousands of words of text that he had never before encountered.

Martin began to read the Bible avidly. As he did so, the deeper issues of life began to assume a new importance, and new doubts and fears began to arise in his mind. Suddenly, heaven and hell became more real to him than ever before. The study of God's word revealed to him his own unfitness, and sowed the seeds of an ever-deepening sense of his sinfulness. All his old childhood fears returned, with a new urgency.

What if he were to die suddenly? Could he face his maker with a peaceful heart and mind? Assuredly not! Martin was too afraid of God's wrath. He was terrified at the thought of having to appear before an almighty judge who might hand down a sentence condemning Martin to endless years of pain and suffering. Now, in his late teens, the idea of his sudden death was only a remote and very unlikely possibility. Or so it had seemed until a near-fatal accident on his way home to Mansfeld at the end of one term.

In common with all students of his day, Martin carried with him a sword to defend himself from thieves whom he might meet on his three-day journey. Scarcely had Martin reached the outskirts of Erfurt when he stumbled over the uneven road and fell sprawling in the dirt, badly cutting his leg with his sword as he did so.

Lying bleeding in the road, Martin feared that his end had come and death would be only the beginning of his agonies.

Luckily, Martin was traveling with a friend, who swiftly ran off to seek aid back at the college. Help arrived in the form of friends who carried him back to the university. The wound was deep and the loss of blood severe. The sword had sliced through an artery and, while Martin had been able to lessen the bleeding, his leg had swollen badly. Martin prayed to the Virgin Mary for help, but it was a surgeon from a nearby town who finally stanched the flow of blood. For two days Martin was close to death, but he eventually rallied.

A short time later, a fellow candidate for the bachelor's degree at his own college died, swiftly followed by a close friend from his immediate circle. A wave of typhoid swept through the city claiming many victims. To Martin, death and judgment suddenly seemed very close at hand.

By this time, Martin was studying for his Master of Arts degree. He found that he could really enjoy the philosophy part of the course. Geometry, mathematics, music, and astronomy constituted his other subjects, and Martin ranked second in a class of seventeen.

At the age of twenty-one, Martin had the world at his feet. All doors were open to him, and there was scarcely any occupation that was barred to him. Martin's father decided that his son should study law and, since Father was paying for his studies, Martin had little option but to take the new copy of *Corpus Juris*, the great legal tome that his father had bought for him, and enter the Faculty of Law.

One July day in 1505, shortly after Martin's graduation with his master's degree, and as he was starting to come to grips with his law studies, the black fear that had been hanging over him grew into anguish and despair.

After ten days at home, Martin was traveling back to his university. He was alone, and above him dark storm clouds were gathering. They seemed to mirror the dark clouds that had been gathering in the heart of his soul. The first drops of rain began to fall, and soon the torrential downpour forced him to seek shelter under an elm tree.

Sheltering beneath a tree was about the worst course of action that Martin could have chosen in a thunderstorm. A blast of lightning split the tree above him, and the tree stood ablaze for an instant against the gray skies.

The thunderbolt knocked Martin flat, half blinding him. One legend says that Martin had a friend with him that day, who was struck dead by the lightning. Whether or not this is true, the fury of the thunderstorm itself was apparently terrifying and awe-inspiring to the young Luther.

The wind twisted the trees into eerie shapes, and Martin remembered his childhood fear of being chased by witches and goblins. Worst of all was the thought of the demons with pitchforks, whom he believed were even now approaching. One glance from God's reproaching eye, and he would spend an eternity in hell.

"Hell, Martin! Yes, hell! Where you will writhe in torment," the ominous rumblings of thunder seemed to say, in a voice like the deep judgment of an angry God. And jagged, tearing lines of lightning across the sky seemed to split the heavens asunder, opening a pathway to the fires of hell that were even now beckoning to him.

"No! No!" begged Martin, clutching at any straw that might save him from a lost eternity. In desperation, he thought of the patron saint of miners, to whom he had often prayed as a child.

"St. Anne, save me! Save me and I will give up my studies. Dear St. Anne . . . save me and . . . I will do anything . . . I will even *become a monk*!"

4

The Frightened Monk

Y ou can't be serious, Martin," said his friends
when he told them of his intentions, back in
the mundane atmosphere of the college pre-
cinct.

"I have made a holy vow, and I have no alternative but to keep it," Martin explained, though he was
by now beginning to feel foolish for having made the
vow in the first place.

"Eat up," said Martin, pointing to the food he'd
provided for his friends as a farewell gesture before
moving into the monastic life. "Eat, drink, and be
merry, for tomorrow I become a monk!" he quipped.

A monk—yes, that was what he wanted. When he
thought about it, he'd much rather have studied theology than law from the beginning. It was only his
father's antipathy toward the clergy that had forced
him into law studies in the first place. Perhaps this
was God's way of overruling his earthly father, and
putting him in the best place to fulfil his heavenly
father's business.

"Who needs a copy of *Corpus Juris*?" he enquired, giving away the great tome that his father had bought for him. Martin had no further need for legal matters, he believed. No, in his mind now was an image, a picture of a ship with the pope and the cardinals at the prow, and the rowers' benches manned by monks, making toward "the blessed shore" of heaven. The waters all around were filled with struggling laymen, many of them drowning in the ocean of life, and only a few surviving by clinging to the ropes that the monks had thrown to them.

In the midst of life we are in death, Martin thought. His only hope lay in renouncing his worldly pursuits and devoting his energies to the service of God. He had to take his place, as soon as possible, at the rowing benches in the comparative safety of that great ship—the church.

There remained just one act to perform before entering the monastery, and it was one which filled him with dread. He was going to have to tell his parents that he intended to give up his career in law. For a moment, Martin wondered whether he might not rather face the Devil himself than face his father with that news. He could imagine how his father's face would redden, how his eyes would narrow and his teeth clench. He could picture how his father would wave his fist in the air with rage.

In the end, Martin decided not to break the news in person. After the monastery gates had closed behind him, he communicated his decision in a short letter. He had been called "by heavenly terrors" to become a monk, he explained to his father. "Not freely or desirously, but walled around with the terror and pain of a sudden death, I vowed a constrained and necessary vow," he wrote.

Now, when Martin had achieved the dignity of Master of Arts at the university, his father had begun to address his son with great dignity and honor. But in the letter that Martin received in reply to his news, his father again addressed him as though he were a disobedient child. His father's reply was the written equivalent of all those beatings that Martin had so often received as a small boy.

The monastery that Martin had joined was of the Augustinian order. It was one of thirty monasteries of that order, which abounded in Germany at that time. The head of the order in Germany was a man named Von Staupitz, and he maintained a high standard of conduct and discipline within the order.

It would be nice to report that the monks welcomed Martin with open arms. But it would not be true. The monks were very choosey about whom they admitted to their order. Early in his induction, Martin was lectured by the prior, Father Lang, about the monastic life, with its deprivations, the labors expected of a novice, the renunciation of the novice's own will, and the all-important vows of poverty, chastity, and obedience.

In accordance with the usual practice, Martin was first admitted to the order simply as a novice. The crown of his head was shaved into the characteristic tonsure of a holy man, and Martin put on a hair shirt and a rough habit, in place of his fine student's clothing, prostrating himself before the other monks.

"Can you live in this way?" the prior asked.

"Yes," came the reply, "with God's help, and to the extent that frailty allows."

Once he had begun the monastic life, the hardships were greater than he had expected. He was sent begging into the streets of Erfurt, where he had so recently ridden on horseback in the torchlight procession that had celebrated his promotion to Master of Arts, until an outcry from the university obliged their former star pupil to beg only in the outlying villages.

"A strange fellow, this new novice," said the other monks. "He brought nothing with him into the monastery save for two Latin books. Well, you can't eat books, can you? Now, if he'd brought us a cheese or a cask of wine . . ."

As a brilliant young student, Martin was a marked man. His superiors were determined that humility should be the first monastic virtue that he would learn. He was given the most menial tasks to perform: waiting on his brothers; sweeping the chapel; cleaning the monks' cells; polishing the steps; and climbing to the top of the bell-tower to wind the clock. But his usual task was to be sent out begging. "Sack on back," the monks would say. Some of them seemed to take delight in humiliating the one who made their own ignorance so conspicuous.

There was consolation for Martin though, in the form of a second letter from his father. Two of Martin's young brothers had died of the plague soon after Hans Luther had written his first letter, and rumors had reached Mansfeld that Martin himself was either ill or already dead. Fearing divine judgment, his father relented. He resigned himself to Martin's decision, "with reluctance and sadness."

As the weeks passed, Martin's nerves were frayed bare by the demands of monastic life. It was a strain to remember all the times of prayer and worship—

seven times each day—and the great manuals for the celebration of the mass, which had to be memorized. The rules of the order were precise and intricate. Some matters had to be confessed in public and others in private. There were places where talking was permitted, and others where strict silence had to be observed. There were times set aside for all the brothers to gather and confess their violation of monastic rules. Punishments would be given out for these violations, and might mean a gesture of penance or a severe flogging before the assembled brotherhood.

Martin's little cell contained only a table, a chair, and a straw bed. Here he spent many hours alone, reading, praying, and meditating. At the end of his one-year probationary period, Martin became a full-fledged lay member of the monastic community. The day came when he put his hand on the *Rules of St. Augustine*, as it lay on the knees of the prior, and swore his final vows of lifetime loyalty to the order, and to God. But the miner's son from Mansfeld soon found that Martin the monk was subject to the same weaknesses, doubts, and despairs that he had felt in the outside world.

Martin continued to spend many hours in prayer and Bible study, but nothing lifted him from the moments of despair and grief that he had always known. He still felt that God was offended with him and that he could never gain His forgiveness. Bitterly, he fought to tame his arrogant and impatient spirit. In order to subjugate his body, he once took a whip and scourged his back and thighs, until his back was bloody, but still he did not feel right with God. He administered another thirty lashes to his bleeding back. Then another thirty. And thirty more. He might have flayed his back raw if unconsciousness had not overpowered him.

The next morning, Brother Martin did not leave his cell. When no reply was given to the repeated calls of the monks outside, his door was forced open, and the young monk was found stretched out upon the floor in a deep stupor. It was said that nothing could revive Martin, until one of the monks stood over him and began singing one of his favorite hymns. The soothing strains gradually returned Martin to consciousness, if not to happiness.

A short while later, Staupitz, the vicar-general of the Augustinian order, chanced to arrive at the monastery on a routine tour of inspection. Martin's wasted form, his sunken eyes and dejected mien attracted Staupitz' attention. The broad-faced and kindly German, deeply read in the Scriptures, arranged for a private interview with Martin.

Martin knelt in the vicar-general's presence, but the older man was not about to stand on ceremony. He treated Martin as an uncle would treat a favorite nephew; and he questioned Martin, it seemed, from a genuine concern for the young monk's well-being.

"I noticed you at the dinner table, Brother Martin. You hardly touched your food."

"Ah, Father, you don't know what I suffer. I despair at what will come of me when I die. I'm terrified at the prospect of having to face almighty God . . ."

"With that kind of fear, you have more need than most of a hearty meal!" Staupitz quipped. "It's a pleasant afternoon. Let's take a walk in the garden. You lead the way," he said as they went outside, "You know it better than I."

Martin was soon engaged in informal conversation with the kindly old gentleman. Staupitz was gratified to learn of Martin's interest in the Scriptures, and the two chatted at great length as they walked.

"When I first opened a Bible, at Erfurt University, I was loath to close it again until I'd read it from cover to cover. But oh, the Scriptures only made my own sins—my faults and failings—more apparent to me. Why, I kept making vows and promises, but I never seemed able to keep them. And only last week . . ."

"Whoa! Steady, Brother Martin. My experience is exactly the same! If I had to keep on being good in order to be vicar-general of this order, I wouldn't last a day. I'm sure there are people in jail who make a better job of being good than I!

"I suppose if we all kept our promises, and were forever doing good deeds, we'd all be jolly pleased with ourselves—and that would be a worse sin! There's no shame in not being 'good'; so stop trying to make a martyr of yourself.

"Brother, you want to be without sin, so you're constantly trying to *find* sins in yourself. You're trying to turn yourself into a story-book 'sinner,' and I fear that you believe in a story-book God, who goes about striking people down with thunderbolts! My son, our God is a God of *love*. Has no one ever told you about Jesus?"

"Oh Father, please don't mention that name," Martin exclaimed. "I'm more frightened of Jesus than I ever was of my teachers or my parents!"

"You have no need to be frightened of Him, Brother Martin," comforted the wise old man. "Jesus is your savior. You can't be right with God through your own actions, but only through what Jesus has done for you. Faith in Jesus achieves more than good works can ever do.

"You're searching for peace, but the peace you need can only come from Jesus.

"But no more now. It will soon be time for vespers, and I must prepare myself. Before you go, my son, is there anything you have lying heavy on your mind that you would like to say to me?"

Martin realized that this was an invitation to make a general confession, if he wished. And Martin confessed. More easily than he had ever done before, he poured out a list of his wrongdoings; but now he realized that his most serious sin was failing to trust in the righteousness of God.

"Remember, Brother Martin, that when you have done wrong, think not on how much you must pay to satisfy your guilt, but how much Jesus paid for you. I must be gone. Peace be with you."

Martin always remembered Staupitz' kind words of encouragement. But encouragement was not the only gift that he gave to Martin. He also gave him the chance to become, not just a monk, but a priest. It was Staupitz' responsibility to decide which of the monks would remain simply as lay brothers, and which would be trained as priests. Martin had been such a talented student before entering the monastery that he was a natural choice for the priesthood.

By this time, Luther had been away from Erfurt University for two years. Now he returned there to continue his schooling. This time though, he was not to study law, but theology. He took courses that led him to the bachelor of arts degree in the Bible. Martin became a sub-deacon, then a deacon, before he was finally allowed to become a priest. His training had taught him that it was possible to know God as a loving father, who loved to forgive His children. This seemed at odds, however, with Martin's ideas of fatherhood as he had observed them in his own father, Hans Luther.

This conflict between what he had been taught about his heavenly Father, and what he knew about his earthly father, was to come to a head as he officiated at his first mass. His natural father would be in attendance; and it would be the first time that he had seen him since he entered the monastery.

On April 3, 1507, the twenty-three-year-old monk was solemnly ordained as a priest, in front of the great altar in Erfurt Cathedral. Martin attained an office which, according to Catholic thinking, would empower him to stand as an intermediary between God and man; to perform the full rites of the mass; to consecrate the bread and wine before the kneeling congregation, and to dispense the body of Christ.

"Receive thou the power of sacrificing for the living and the dead!" said the presiding bishop. That the holy Catholic church should have believed itself to have the right to confer the power to do any such thing was, Martin thought in his later years, unutterable blasphemy. "I wonder," he said long afterward, "that the earth did not open up and swallow me!"

Shortly thereafter, came the great festival that was to open his priestly career. On May 2, Martin was to say his first mass. He had not yet found peace with his heavenly Father, and he found it excruciatingly difficult to face his earthly father. Hans Luther had arrived the previous day, with a company of twenty horsemen and a handsome gift for the monastery.

The tolling of the monastery bell began the day as

the honored guests crossed the cobbled courtyard and took their places in church. Then the monks entered, chanting a psalm. At last the moment came when Martin stood alone before the high altar. The words that he had read in some pious textbook came back to him: "Oh, truly heavenly indulgence! Oh, cumulative grace! What super-excellent glory of the priest to hold and to disperse his God, distributing Him to others!" Oh, woefully inadequate Martin!

Trembling as he pronounced the Latin formulation, he worried that perhaps he was not correctly robed, or that he was not pronouncing the words properly. At last the moment came when Martin was expected to transform the bread and wine into the body of Christ, sacrifice it on the altar, and offer it up in the presence of almighty God. Yes, that was all that was needed. Easy enough, wasn't it? "A simple conjuring trick," whispered a voice in one ear. *Martin! It's blasphemy!* screamed a voice in his other ear.

"I am dust and ashes and full of sin, and not worthy to be a priest" were the words that he kept repeating in his mind. He feared that he would be overcome by a manic fit. He would desecrate the body of Christ with obscene words and gestures, while his father smiled grimly.

But no. The loving God, whom he feared as the Devil in hell, was even at that moment forgiving Martin for his fears. He was forgiving, loving, supporting, and comforting Martin in his hour of need. God was giving freely of himself, forgiving Martin's misguided thoughts, and assuring him that no one present was aware of the doubts that were passing through Martin's mind.

Soon, Martin was distributing the bread to his fellow monks, and to the distinguished visitors. What did Martin feel when he placed a piece of bread—the consecrated "host" as it was known—into his father's mouth? Was he perhaps expecting his father to jump up and shout, "It's a fraud! You've not done it! This is still bread!" Perhaps. But Martin's first mass went off without incident.

Afterward, Martin joined his father and the other monks at a celebratory dinner. What Martin needed most from his father were a few simple words of encouragement: "Well done, son. I'm proud of you." But his father seemed totally unmoved.

"Dear Father, why were you so against my becoming a monk? Perhaps you have now changed your mind," said Martin, fishing for some hint of understanding and acceptance. "See, the life is so quiet and godly."

"You learned scholar!" shouted Hans angrily. "Have you never read in the Bible that you should honor your father and your mother? And now you have left me and your mother to look after ourselves in our old age!"

Martin wished that the earth would open up beneath his feet, and hide him from his father's wrath.

As the other monks began to remonstrate with Hans—after all, the Bible also commanded that *God* must be honored above all else, even above one's parents—Hans turned on his son and spat out a venomous jibe:

"God grant that it wasn't the Devil you met with in that thunderstorm, that drove you to your vow!" And, with that, all Martin's doubts engulfed him. What if it *was* the Devil that had wanted him to become a monk?

If the monastic life could get a man into heaven; *if* the bread and wine became the body and blood of Christ; *if* Martin had faith; *if* Martin loved God; *if* Martin did good works—then he need not worry. But what if none of these were true or possible?

5

The Frightened Teacher

I 've been sleepless for a long time," Martin told his prior, Father Lang. "Night after night, I lie awake pondering my sins, and fearing that the Devil will come and carry me off."

"Brother Martin, I thought we'd been through all of this before," sighed the old prior. "Do you not believe in the forgiveness of sins?"

"Well yes. I believe it, because it says so in the Creed."

"I mean the forgiveness, not the payment for sins," said Father Lang. "It seems to me that you're trying to earn your way into heaven, instead of accepting God's pardon and forgiveness."

"I hope to be forgiven, of course."

"And so you shall! Stop worrying so much," urged Martin's superior. "It's not God who is frowning on you; it's you who are frowning on God. Now, I have some good news for you. Von Staupitz, our vicar-general, is sending you to Wittenberg."

"Wittenberg?"

"Yes, you know that Duke Frederick of Saxony has begun a new university there? Well, apparently funds for buildings, books, and teachers are in short supply, so our vicar-general has offered several monks to be teachers. You're one of them."

"But, Father Lang—"

"Brother Martin!" the old man cut him short. "I do not want to hear any more about how unworthy you feel yourself to be! Did you, or did you not, swear a vow of obedience when you entered this order?"

"But of course . . ."

"Well how about keeping that vow instead of being so disagreeable?" the old man smiled. "You're going to Wittenberg to be a teacher, and that's the end of it."

So Martin went off to be a teacher. But that was far from the end of it.

Some of the local monks were not sorry to see Martin leave. His piety had not always made him popular among the brothers. In nearby monasteries and convents, Luther's name was a byword for pomposity. He was too aloof, too scholarly, too moody, and too fond of sleepless vigils and prolonged fasts, they felt. His name was frequently bandied about as a monk who was more devout and more pious than St. Peter himself. But Martin had also made many friends at Erfurt who were sorry to see him go. Martin would look back on these old friends and old times with affection.

Over at Wittenberg, Duke Frederick brooded over his new university like a mother hen. To his new offspring he was as generous as his purse would afford, though his good intentions often fell short in actual performance. Still, one way or another, with the monasteries, the town, and the great Castle Church all chipping in, the university was beginning to acquire the buildings, books, and teachers that it needed.

Wittenberg was about seventy miles to the northeast of Erfurt, and was the main city of Saxony—the region of Germany over which Duke Frederick was ruler. It was a walled city of scarcely more than 2,000 inhabitants, and—compared with Erfurt—it was out in the sticks.

Martin must have wondered what he was letting himself in for as he crossed the moat and entered the town for the first time. "A stinking sand-dune," one contemporary called the town. It had a monastery at one end, and Duke Frederick's castle at the other. Along the town's two main streets ran two brooks, though they were more like stinking sewers. A dung-hill of a marketplace lay at the town's center, next to the main lecture hall of the new university.

Staupitz himself was Professor of Biblical Theology, while Luther was expected to lecture on the *Nicomachean Ethics of Aristotle*—a renowned work of philosophy. Aristotle, of course, was a famous Greek philosopher—but Martin found his work singularly unimpressive. "That jackanapes who had made a fool of the church," Martin called him.

A few days after his arrival, Martin made his way to the Castle Church, under the daunting shadow of Duke Frederick's fortress. Von Staupitz, who was now Martin's firm friend, showed him the town's greatest attraction.

"Within these boxes, Brother Martin, are the holy

relics that the duke and his ancestors have collected over the years," said Staupitz. The relics were divided into eight lots, and were kept in eight separate corridors.

"Here are 1,838 items from blessed martyrs, and 331 from Christ himself," Staupitz enthused. "This box contains pieces of the true cross—the cross on which our Lord was crucified. Here is a vial of milk from the bosom of the Blessed Virgin herself . . ."

As Staupitz led him along the winding corridors, showing him each of the relics, Martin became increasingly restless and ill at ease. Could any of these items actually be genuine? Why, there were enough "fragments of the true cross" in abbeys and monasteries throughout Europe to make a dozen crosses! Were these dry old bones really those of the Holy Innocents—the children of Bethlehem whom Herod had senselessly slain 1500 years ago? They could have come from the graveyard in Mansfeld and no one would be any the wiser! Was this really straw from the manger in which the infant Jesus had lain? It didn't look more than a year old, let alone fifteen centuries!

"And this is one of the forty pieces of silver for which our Lord was betrayed, Brother Martin. And here, the thigh bone of St. Peter . . ."

There were at least five other thigh bones of St. Peter in Germany alone. St. Peter must have been a funny shape if he had so many thigh bones!

"Here, Brother Martin!" said Staupitz with particular excitement, "See! A piece of cloth, spun by Jesus' mother!"

It looked a bit decrepit, Martin thought. Surely all these so-called relics must be fakes!

"Brother, is something the matter?"

"Can these really be genuine?" pondered Martin. "And even if they are, what then?"

"Dear Brother," said Staupitz solemnly, "a person entering the basilica where these relics are housed gains an indulgence of 1,443 years remission of purgatory."

The Catholic church believed, at that time, that the forgiveness of sins or wrongdoing, was a fourfold process. First the sinner had to confess, or admit to the wrongdoing. The second step was called repentance, or turning one's back on the action that had been sinful, though the church thought of it in terms of "doing penance" for wrongdoing. The other two steps were called the satisfaction of sins, the actual "paying for" the wicked deed; and the absolution, or assurance of forgiveness. The order of the last two parts could be reversed, but the sin had still to be paid for, the church believed.

Often, a priest hearing confession would set a penance, or penalty for the sin. It might be a public flogging, or going without food for several days. The church believed that any wrongdoing that was not confessed and paid for in this way would have to be paid for after death, in a place of torment called purgatory.

Purgatory! The very name made Martin quail! The only way to avoid suffering the pain of purgatory was through penances. These penances were basically "good works," though the church's idea of a "good work" left a lot to be desired. It basically consisted of doing something either boring or unpleasant. Going on a pilgrimage was reckoned to be a good work; so was visiting a holy place. Duke Frederick had amassed so many relics that his Castle Church qualified as a "holy place," with 1,443 years remission of purgatory attached to it; though only one visit per person per year was allowed to qualify for the remission. Even many visits to the Castle Church would make little impact on the total sentence, since the church taught that most people would have to spend millions of years in purgatory when they died!

"Brother Martin, it hardly matters whether these relics are genuine. It matters only that the people *believe* them to be genuine, and are brought nearer to the presence of God through their contemplations."

It was all a ploy to make people go to church, and Staupitz felt that the end justified the means. But Martin, while believing that coming closer to God was a laudable aspiration, if it could be achieved, was not at all sure that the worship of relics was a good method. In fact, at this time, Martin was not at all sure about *anything*!

"Am I sinning through my lack of faith in these relics?" Martin wondered aloud. "If so, then I should confess immediately."

"No, Brother Martin," Staupitz said. He was the person to whom Martin usually made his confessions, and the last time they had met, Martin had spent six hours telling him of his largely imagined wrongdoings.

"I've heard every detail of your confession this week, Martin, and I already know all your faults. Didn't we spend most of yesterday discussing them? No, don't come to confession again until you've lapsed into some really big sin, that's important enough to confess.

"Don't torture yourself with your sins. Throw

yourself into the Savior's arms—the Savior who died for you."

Staupitz had come to know Martin well. What to some would seem pure thoughts and deeds, Martin would analyze into various impure ones. Where his actions were virtuous, he found impious motives. He had little self-confidence, and needed to be bullied into doing what he wanted to do all along, otherwise he would think himself presumptuous and self-seeking.

"Next week, Martin, you are going to preach publicly," Staupitz said bluntly.

"I dare not," said Martin, thinking of the solemn responsibility.

"You must! I command you," said Staupitz, no longer simply Martin's friend but also his superior, to whom he had sworn an oath of obedience.

"If I do, I shall die," said Martin, playing for Staupitz' sympathy. But the wily old vicar-general saw through the ruse:

"So what? The Lord requires faithful servants in heaven, as well as on earth! You know the little church in the public square?"

"That tiny wooden church, so dilapidated that it has to be propped up by timbers?"

"Yes, the one with the pulpit made of rough boards. You won't become very proud or conceited preaching in there, will you? That should shorten your next confession! If the place isn't beautiful, it will soon be beautified by your doctrine."

And so Martin began his public preaching ministry. Within weeks, the little barn-like church became too small for the throngs that were attracted by Martin's powerful, direct teaching. Under Staupitz' influence, Martin was beginning to come into real knowledge of the heavenly Father of whom he had been so afraid. But his growth in faith was soon to suffer a serious setback.

In 1510, Staupitz arranged a pleasant diversion for Martin. The old monk had thought long and hard about the idea of introducing one single set of rules and regulations to govern the running of all the Augustinian monasteries in Germany. It would solve a lot of the minor problems and disputes that had been taking up the vicar-general's time lately. The problem was that not all the monasteries wanted the rules to be merged. To settle the dispute, someone would have to make the journey to Rome, and that someone—the dissident monks decided—would be Martin Luther. Though Staupitz was not pleased with the divisions in the order, he enthusiastically gave Martin his leave and goodwill to journey to Rome to have the matter finally decided by the pope.

In November 1510, Martin and a fellow monk named Dr. Johann Nathin began the 850-mile walk to Rome, taking them through the windswept mountain passes of the snow-covered Alps. On occasion, they had to sleep outdoors, though usually they were able to reach a friendly monastery along the way, and refresh themselves. For many weeks they traveled, until finally the Eternal City, as Rome was known, came into view.

"Greetings to you, Holy Rome!" Martin shouted in the exuberance of reaching his journey's end. But exuberance soon turned to despair and despondency.

Here, at the hub of the world, where the church's ruler, Pope Julius II lived, were several monasteries and dozens of churches. Surely it would be a wonderful place, its streets spilling over with Christians of all nationalities, all at one with God and each other, Martin had thought.

Sadly, Rome was not like that at all. Everywhere he looked, Martin found the church rotten with vice and corruption. A stay at one of the monasteries in Milan, on the way down to Rome, had given him an inkling of what to expect. He had been annoyed and amazed at the extravagance of the monks. They lived in rooms lined with marble and adorned with costly paintings. Instead of coarse habits and hair shirts, they wore immaculately tailored clothing cut from expensive cloth. Martin had been particularly horrified when, on Friday, the day when the monks were supposed to eat frugally, they ate more meat and rich delicacies than on any other day!

Rome was even worse. Here, many of the cardinals lived in open sin with their mistresses. The streets were narrow and dirty. Cattle and sheep grazed on the ancient ruin of the city once famed for its splendor. The pope himself often had to take refuge in his castle, for fear of the violence on the streets.

"The chief of police rides around the town every night with a patrol of 300 men. Anyone caught in the streets after dark bearing arms is either hanged, drowned in the River Tiber, or tortured," Martin was told.

Great painters like Raphael and Michelangelo were working in the city at the time and, though Martin never met them, he may have seen the ceiling of the Sistine Chapel as Michelangelo's great work was being executed. A few years earlier, Leonardo Da Vinci had painted his most famous work—the *Mona Lisa*.

Pope Julius was not available to trouble himself with Martin's business. Sadly, he thought more of money and fighting than of religion. His armies were at war with France, and Martin heard it said that, after the French troops had defeated his army at Ravenna, the pope had thrown down his prayerbook with the blasphemous oath: "So, God, you too are a Frenchman?"

The priests in Rome made a mockery of the gospel, almost competing with each other to see who could complete the most masses within one hour. Martin was horrified to see the sacrament abused in this way.

Like all visitors to Rome, Martin was careful to visit all the shrines, with their holy relics—which he had been taught would do so much for his soul. Most famous of these relics was the *Scala Sancta*, or sacred stairs, at the Lateran church. These were reputed to be the stairs from Pontius Pilate's palace, which Jesus had ascended when presented for judgment.

Martin ascended these twenty-eight steps on his hands and knees, saying a *Paternoster* (Lord's Prayer) on each one, and even kissing each step for good measure. Some believed that each prayer said on these steps released a soul from purgatory. As he climbed, Martin almost wished his parents were dead so that he could give them such a favor. But when he reached the top he stood up and said aloud: "Who knows whether it is true?"

Indeed, how did anyone—let alone Martin Luther, a monk from a provincial backwater—know if anything were true? All the corruption that he had seen in Rome had soured him against the church and God; yet he still feared for his soul. Could he never be right with God? The ordinary people believed that in visiting the shrines where relics were housed, or climbing the sacred stairs on their knees, they were earning forgiveness of sins—and the clergy encouraged them in this false belief. "Where's the justice in that?" thought Martin, who could not find it in his heart to love or respect the One he thought responsible for so much falsehood and misery.

"Love God?" questioned Martin. "I hate Him!"

6

An End to Fear

Love God? I hate Him!" Martin repeated, after his return from Rome. But the old man whom Martin thought would be shocked by the statement was unshaken. Staupitz stroked his chin and turned to Martin, who was sitting next to him under the pear tree in the monastery garden at Wittenberg.

"Surely it's not God whom you hate, but His church," said Staupitz, making a wry distinction.

"Aye, if there's a hell, then Rome stands on it," retorted Martin. "Perhaps I am unjust to blame God for the deficiencies of His church."

"I would say so, Brother. You complain that whoever came to Rome bringing money went away forgiven of their sins. I fear that you went to Rome 'with your onions,' but returned bearing the stench of garlic!"

The two friends bantered with one another for some time, with Staupitz gradually helping Martin to clarify his thoughts. Yes, thought Staupitz, here is an intelligent scholar. The old vicar-general would soon have to relinquish the post of Professor of Biblical Theology at Wittenberg, and he felt that Martin Luther was the logical successor. The only problem lay in convincing Martin that he was the man for the job.

"God needs men like you in His church if He is to stop the rot that is discrediting Christianity," said Staupitz. Then, taking a deep breath, he added: "God needs you as a professor—as a Doctor of the Scriptures. You must set yourself to teaching the Bible—"

"But . . ." began Martin, as Staupitz had expected; Martin continued until he had expounded fifteen good reasons why he should not become a doctor. Wise old Staupitz waited until he had had his say, then countered each of his arguments with sound common sense. He knocked down reason after reason. One of Martin's strongest objections was that he couldn't afford the fees that were required for the course of study that he would need before taking on such a responsible office.

"Duke Frederick has already agreed to pay your fees," said Staupitz, who had obviously been mapping out Martin's future while Martin was in Rome. "Now, say no more. I am your superior and I lay my commands upon you."

Martin was still a young man in turmoil, yet he willingly obeyed his superior. For a start, the alternative would have been to return to the monastery at Erfurt and, though Erfurt was a thriving metropolis in comparison with Wittenberg, the failure of Martin's mission to Rome had left him none too popular at Erfurt.

The idea of Martin studying for a doctorate at Wittenberg rather than Erfurt caused some consternation at his old university. There was a rivalry between the two seats of learning and the Erfurt authorities frowned on Wittenberg as an upstart young university. It was Dr. Nathin, who had accompanied Martin to Rome, who cut through the red tape. The Dean of Erfurt was droning drowsily away, reading lengthy extracts from the university regulations, when Dr. Nathin exploded impatiently. He interrupted the Dean, reading from a roll of paper a list of textbooks that Martin would be expected to read.

"You can't interrupt me!" barked the Dean.

"I just have!" laughed Dr. Nathin.

A lively scene ensued and, amid all the fuss, nobody remembered that Martin was supposed to have solemnly promised to do his doctorate only at Erfurt. By the time the Dean realized what had happened, Martin had already completed his doctorate at Wittenberg!

"Beautiful! Beautiful!" wrote Martin in the margins of the great works of St. Augustine and Peter Lombard, which he was required to study. Many other writers did not so endear themselves to Martin. William of Occam, Duns Scotus, Pierre D'Ailly, and Gabriel Biel were all respected authors with whom Martin disagreed.

By October 1512, Martin had passed all the rigorous tests for the Doctor of Theology degree. He invited many of his old friends from Erfurt to attend the colorful ceremony where he would formally receive the honor. What the students from Erfurt must have whispered behind his back would probably have made Martin's ears burn. At Erfurt, he would have had to study for at least ten years before receiving his doctor's degree; but at Wittenberg, he had satisfied all the requirements in less than five.

Proudly, Staupitz—as vicar-general of the Augustinian order and Professor of Biblical Studies—conferred the Doctor's cap on his friend in the course of the ceremony. As Doctor Martin Luther left the church after receiving the honor, he was suddenly accosted from behind. In a moment he had been seized by his arms and legs, and was swung off his feet!

Was this the Erfurt academics about to take their revenge for slighting them, and completing his studies in half the usual time? Perhaps, for a moment, Martin feared that these were the demons with pitchforks that had waited till his greatest academic achievement before carrying him down to the fires of hell!

But if he did, he need not have worried. In an instant, Martin felt himself being lifted into the air. It was his fellow students who had seized him, and then proudly placed him on their shoulders and carried him through the streets, while the town bell added its note of congratulations.

At the age of twenty-eight, the pattern of Martin's life appeared to be set. He would lecture twice a week, every week, to progressive generations of students at Wittenberg, until he became so old and feeble that he could only croak out his last lecture.

The courses that he now began to teach were a constant source of pleasure. Previously he had taught philosophy, but now he was reunited with his first love—theology. Martin was a scrupulously dutiful lecturer. Though his students may have found him quirky and pedantic at times, he was a popular professor. Martin loved to debate with his students on the finer points of theological issues. This debating forced him further and further into his study of the original Greek and Hebrew in which the Bible was written. There, digging like a persistent and methodical miner, he finally struck pay-dirt. In those times of private study between lectures, Martin was at the same time bidding farewell to one age and assisting in the birth of a new age.

The breakthrough occurred one very ordinary day, when Martin was in his private office—a room on the second floor of a tower attached to the Augustinian monastery at Wittenberg. He was preparing to preach and lecture on Paul's letter to the Romans. Methodically reading through the letter, he came upon the passage that was to put an end to his fears forever.

"I am not ashamed of the Gospel," Martin read, pondering the words of the apostle Paul. "It is the power of God for salvation to everyone who has faith, to the Jew first, and also to the Greek. For in it the righteousness of God is revealed, through faith, for faith. As it is written, 'The righteous shall live by faith' " (Romans 1:16, 17).

Well, thought Martin, *the first part is easy enough to understand; it simply says that God's Word, the gospel, shows the way of deliverance from eternal death. But what about this bit: the righteousness of God?*

The very idea filled him with panic! Still a guilt-obsessed sinner, Martin felt a deep fear and hostility toward those words. *Surely if God is just, then Martin Luther is damned*, he thought. He had confessed his sins, repented—turned from the things that he had done wrong—and confessed again; but there was no way he could *make* God forgive him.

When Martin had lectured on Psalm 31, he had quickly passed on when he reached the line: "Deliver me in thy righteousness." Every night for years, though his students had not realized it, their professor was battling in his tower room with the Devil.

"The righteousness of God" had tormented Martin from the very beginning of his studies. What did it really mean? When he talked to Staupitz about the matter, sitting under the old pear tree, his mentor told him that "repentance is not genuine unless it begins with a love of righteousness and God."

Staupitz' words struck Martin like a "sharp arrow of the Almighty," and he began to compare them with the rest of the Scriptures that teach penitence. Where his knowledge of Greek had improved sufficiently, he realized that the actual meaning of the word was "to repent, or turn one's back on wrongdoing," rather than "to do penance—by fasting, pilgrimages, praying to saints, etc."

But God shows His righteousness by punishing sinners every time that they do wrong, Martin kept saying to himself. *He shows His righteousness by punishing me, sinner that I am! The only way a man can become righteous is to do all that God wants him to do . . . isn't it?*

Martin stopped, suddenly.

No, that can't be right!

Then he realized he'd been wrong all those years! God wasn't cruel and harsh at all!

St. Paul says that man is made righteous—or just—by believing in something that God has done for him. But what has God done for man to make him righteous or holy?

He sent Jesus Christ to make us holy! Jesus kept the law perfectly, and yet He was punished by being put to death. He had not done anything wrong, but I have!

That's it! God punished Jesus in my place, by letting His own son be punished by death. Now I am holy in God's sight because I know and believe that Jesus is righteous and holy for me, and He has taken my punishment!

Yes, Martin had finally realized how he could be sure that God would forgive him. Whereas he had previously thought of God as a stern father, like his own natural father, Martin now saw Him as loving and gracious, ready to reach out and forgive him—and to help him through his life—if he only had faith and believed with a confident surrender and a firm reliance.

I feel as though I have been reborn and gone through open gates into paradise, Martin thought.

If God had been prepared to forgive sinful man without requiring some penalty, He would have been very undependable, and that lack of steadfast resolve would have made Him a very frightening and unpredictable deity. He would have been like an unpredictable schoolmaster who rewards or punishes a pupil depending on how He feels at a particular moment, rather than because of the pupil's performance.

One of the clearest illustrations of how God combines justice and mercy can be found in an old story about an important judge who presided at the trial of a man who had committed a serious crime. As the trial progressed, it became more and more obvious that the accused was guilty. Then it became known that the accused was a childhood friend of the judge.

Everybody expected the accused to get let off with a light sentence, because of the long friendship, but when the judge finally pronounced judgment, the whole court was stunned to hear the most severe sentence possible! The convicted man would have to pay a very large fine, or spend many years in prison. There seemed to be no way in which he could raise enough money, so prison seemed to be the only option.

Then the judge rose before the court. He took off his powdered wig, his ermine robes, and all the trappings of his office. He left his place of honor at the head of the court and walked down to the lowest station. There, he walked up to the clerk of the court and paid, with his own money, the enormous fine that he himself had imposed only a few moments earlier!

If he had let off the guilty person, he would have been a corrupt and unworthy judge. But by paying the fine himself the letter of the law had been upheld and his love for his childhood friend had been expressed in the most costly and loving manner imaginable.

That was precisely what Martin Luther had discovered about God. The righteousness of God had demanded that a sinner could not be let off unpunished. But God's abundant love had required him to pay the penalty himself. All Martin had to do was to have faith that God had indeed paid the price, and he could be forgiven. Not only that, but God's righteousness would become the sinner's righteousness. Martin Luther could be righteous!

How the tears must have trickled down Martin's face when he reached that revelation. God was no longer a terrifying, vengeful figure, but a kind, wonderful person. Martin remembered the elm tree in the thunderstorm that had caused him to take his vow to become a monk. But it was no longer a vision of terror and wrath. Martin seemed to see it instead—in the lightning flash, asserting its life in every shining leaf—echoing the thunderclap's proclamation: "The righteous shall live by faith!"

"We do not become righteous by doing righteous deeds, but having become righteous we do good works," Martin started to preach to the people of Wittenberg. His students began to sense the spark of faith that glowed brighter and brighter in his heart, and they flocked to his lectures until other professors complained. Martin seemed to be on fire for God. He startled all who heard him by the way he applied the words of the Bible, written more than 1,400 years earlier, to the lives of the people of his own day. Christianity suddenly seemed more alive and relevant than it ever had before.

As Martin became less morose and more outgoing, he was given further responsibilities by Staupitz. Staupitz himself had been sent to Holland to collect more relics for Duke Frederick. Luther undertook the visitation of the monasteries in the vicar-general's absence.

"I'm terribly busy," Martin wrote in a letter to a friend. "I really could do with two secretaries. I seem to do nothing all day but write letters. I also preach at the monastery, preside at mealtimes, and take services in the parish church. I'm keeping an eye on eleven other monasteries, lecturing on St. Paul's letters, and collecting material for my book on the Psalms."

Martin exercised his oversight of the monasteries with love and compassion. Once, when a renegade monk took refuge in a monastery in Mainz, he wrote to the prior there in touching terms:

> The sad news has reached me that one of my brothers from the monastery at Dresden has gone far astray and has fled to you for refuge. I regret that the whole affair was so disgraceful. Nevertheless, I am happy that you were honorable and helpful in taking him in, and have made it possible to end his shame.
>
> He is a lost sheep and belongs in the fold. It is my duty to seek him out and to turn him from the error of his ways, if the Lord Jesus is willing. I therefore beg you, most reverent Father and Prior, if it is in any way possible for you to help, to send him back to Dresden or Wittenberg.
>
> Persuade him to come himself; treat him so kindly that he will come of his own wish. I shall welcome him with open arms. He has nothing to fear. I am aware that great sins happen; it is nothing unusual when a man goes wrong. The miracle occurs when he comes to his senses again. An angel once sinned, even in heaven. So did Adam in paradise. St. Peter fell. Every day a cedar of Lebanon topples to the ground. So there is nothing unusual if a reed is blown here and there by the wind.

What a wonderfully compassionate letter! God had put an end to Martin's fears, and made him righteous. Now, Martin was beginning to do good works; in particular, he was offering mercy and kindness toward a renegade monk—"a lost sheep who belongs in the fold."

Martin himself was once a lost sheep who was found by God. "I was astray for a long time," Martin wrote. "My inner condition was a mystery to me." Now he was spreading the good news—and showing through his actions—that God can always be trusted to find homes for His lost sheep.

7

The Wittenberg Door

The gospel light that Martin had found in his tower room grew from a flickering ember to a roaring blaze as the years passed. Though speaking out plainly against sin, he loved sinners and offered them God's righteousness as the only solution to man's inherent wickedness.

Martin was a sober and steadfast advocate of the truth, and he once caused a hubbub in an academic debate (or "disputation" as it was known in those days) by claiming that a book entitled *True and False Confession*, supposedly written by St. Augustine, was actually a forgery!

"Nonsense, Martin!" shouted Dr. Andreas Karlstadt, the Dean of Wittenberg, Martin's close colleague. Karlstadt tore off to Leipzig to consult a copy of the book, anxious to prove Martin wrong, but returned essentially converted to Martin's position. Karlstadt was now "more Lutheran than Luther," his colleagues began to quip.

Even in mechanical aids for teaching, Martin was

a pioneer. He had sections of St. Paul's letters specially printed with only a few lines to the page, so that there would be plenty of space for his pupils to write notes around them. He showed his consideration and thoughtfulness in many ways, often meticulously copying out his classroom notes neatly so that others might read them easily.

Expounding the Bible at sixteenth-century universities was a leisurely business. One of Martin's contemporaries at Leipzig took twenty-two years to expound the first eight chapters of Jeremiah! In four years, Martin worked his way steadily through the Psalms and two of the letters of St. Paul. He was so illuminating in his lectures on the letters, that he had to keep reminding his students: "I am not the apostle Paul, but only the lecturer on him!"

Toward the end of 1516, a wave of bubonic plague reached Wittenberg and many people disappeared from the town—either to places of safety, or more permanent resting places. Martin wrote a letter to his old friend Lang, who had been his prior at Erfurt:

"Where shall I fly? The world won't come to an end when Brother Martin dies. I shall send the brothers away, if the plague gets worse. I am stationed here and I may not run away because of my vow of obedience, until the same authority which bids me stay commands me to depart. (He was referring to Staupitz.) Not that I do not fear the plague, but I hope that the Lord will deliver me from my fear." Martin was apparently more worried about the harm that his own fear could cause than he was of the plague itself.

The plague passed, and the inhabitants returned. But the storm clouds were gathering over Wittenberg and all over Germany. Martin would be the one to disperse those clouds, and in so doing he would shake the whole world. While Martin was lecturing on theology, and striving—in his own small way—to be a reformer of university studies, God was preparing much bigger fish for him to fry.

The old pope had died in 1513, and a new man, Pope Leo X, had attained the high office. Leo was a connoisseur of the arts. He had many of the finest painters, sculptors, and poets brought to his court. Michelangelo slaved for years producing work to please Leo's merest whim. While Raphael completed his designs for tapestries for the Sistine chapel, Leo could often be found sitting there, beneath Michelangelo's ceiling, listening to the finest singers from France or Greece singing their wonderful church music.

Leo had only been elected pope by political intrigue. When the conclave of cardinals had met to elect Pope Julius's successor, they had become deadlocked. According to custom, the cardinals had been sealed into part of the Vatican palace, and could not leave until they had elected a new pope. As the vapors from the torches and the odor from the lavatory became intolerable, it became clear that a new pope would have to be elected quickly. Fearful of the disease they might contract from their unhygienic conditions, the conclave finally elected Leo as a political expediency. He was not their favorite candidate, but rumor had spread that Leo was on his deathbed. Electing him as pope would buy time for more political in-fighting which, hopefully, would ensure a better and more popular pope next time around.

Unfortunately, Pope Leo X was not on his deathbed. The obese, short-legged cardinal had apparently staged his "illness" as a ruse to get himself elected! On his accession, Leo had not even been a priest. He had had to be ordained and consecrated bishop prior to his enthronement as pope. "He is indeed gross," wrote one of Leo's contemporaries. "He is always in a sweat, and never does anything in the midst of his ceremonial duties but wipe away the perspiration dripping from his face and head and throat and hands with a small linen cloth."

It was not as though Leo had much time for his church duties, which he found tedious. He was much more fond of hunting, and thought nothing of inviting 1,000 or 2,000 select friends to accompany him. Often, he would invite the cardinals in for a game of cards, always gambling for large amounts of money. Leo would always delight his spectators by throwing them his winnings. Leo doubled the spending of his predecessors and brought the Vatican to new depths of decadence.

Of course that sort of lifestyle was very expensive to maintain. "It would be easier," a contemporary remarked, "for a stone to fly than for this pope to keep together 1,000 ducats." And so, every morning before he rose from his bed, Leo would ponder which abbacies and bishoprics were to be conferred; for each time Leo created a new bishop or abbot, the holder of the office would have to pay the pope some recompense for his office. These important offices, naturally, never went to the most qualified person, nor to the person that God wanted, but simply to the person with the most money.

The most important church office in Martin Luther's native Germany was that of the Archbishop of Mainz. Albert of Brandenberg, who already held the offices of Bishop of Halberstadt and Bishop of Magdeberg, hoped to add this third office and make himself head of the Catholic church in Germany.

It was not officially permitted for one person to hold more than one bishopric at a time, let alone three; and Albert was only twenty-three years old—below the age required for a bishop. But this wasn't going to stop Albert. With help from his brother Joachim, he was able to offer Leo sufficient money for these matters to be "overlooked" and for Albert to be appointed the Archbishop of Mainz.

Albert's problem was that he didn't have the money that he had promised to Leo. In desperation, he turned to the Fuggers, a banking family, and borrowed the money.

Albert was now in the position of having to repay an enormous loan. Leo also needed money desperately, for his ambition was to build an enormous new church in Rome—St. Peter's Basilica—which he was determined would be the most beautiful church in the world. Common greed made strong allies of Albert and Leo.

It was finally agreed that Pope Leo X, as head of the church, would grant an indulgence to be sold in Germany to raise the money. Half the proceeds would go to Leo to help build his basilica; and the other half would go to repaying Albert's debts.

An indulgence was a formal letter from the pope, usually bearing his seal, which proposed to take away the need for payment for sin. These indulgences formed a part of the church's teaching on repentance and forgiveness. The church, as we have seen, taught that to receive forgiveness four things were needed: the penitent had to be truly sorry; the sins had to be confessed to a priest; the priest had to formally forgive the sinner; good works had to be done to prove that the confession and repentance were genuine.

But contrast this teaching with the Bible's teaching on the matter—the teaching followed by the early church, and which Martin had recently rediscovered for himself. In this teaching the penitent has to be truly sorry and to turn away from the things that he knows to be wrong. The sins have to be confessed to God, which can be done in silent prayer as effectively as to a priest. God is ready and willing to forgive sins. The penitent can then be made right with God (or justified by God's favor—grace), through the penitent's faith that Jesus died in order to pay the price of sin. Faith normally leads to a natural willingness to do good works. But performing these good works is not essential for forgiveness.

The discrepancies are obvious. The trouble with the true biblical position, based on the teachings of Christ, and which Martin embraced, was that the church couldn't make any money out of it! Of course, Christ had never intended that being one of His followers should be financially rewarding. But for hundreds of years, corrupt popes had had other ideas.

It's likely that the true biblical (or evangelical) position was glimpsed by many church scholars, even when the abuses were most rampant. But the true position had never really percolated down very far. The average parish priest followed the church's corrupt teaching in the belief that this was the true teaching. Even Martin's studies to become a Doctor of Theology had not shown him the error. Staupitz perhaps was aware of the errors, but he had not broken through to the truth. Perhaps Staupitz was not even aware that the mistaken views were filling the minds of most of the parish priests. Or perhaps he *was* aware, but was afraid to do anything about it, looking instead to Martin as the St. George who would slay the dragon of false teachings.

It was because of the church's mistaken view that indulgences came into existence. The church had initially proclaimed that the good works it believed to be essential for forgiveness, which were *not* performed in this life, would have to be done in purgatory, after death. All the wrongs that people had committed, and which had not been punished, would have to be paid for in that awful place.

People in Luther's day were not, in general, afraid of hell. They believed, rightly, that they were assured of a place in heaven as long as they sincerely repented of all their wrongdoing, accepted the teaching that Christ had died to make it possible for them to be forgiven, and lived their lives in a Christ-like manner. It was only the thought of purgatory that frightened them. They might have to endure thousands, even millions of years of punishment before they could taste the joys of heaven.

After the church had taught this doctrine—which is not found in the Bible, and which is totally contrary to Christ's teaching—they taught that there was only one alternative. This was to receive the benefits of the Treasury of Grace.

The Roman Catholic concept of this treasury of grace was of a bank in which were deposited the good works of Christ, the saints, and all believers. People who fell short of a good life, and had not done enough good deeds, could draw on this treasury as though it were a bank account. The paper indulgence acted like a check.

Originally, indulgences were slips of paper that could be bought, and which would give remission of the time that had to be endured in purgatory. But the common people saw indulgences simply as pieces of paper that they could buy that would in themselves forgive their sins; and this was a gross trivialization of the gospel.

What was worse, many people interpreted this as forgiveness for future sins as well as past sins. A man who owned an indulgence might believe that it was not wrong to steal or murder, because he already owned a document signed and sealed stating that his sins were forgiven.

Initially, the sale of indulgences had been done to finance the Crusades; but as time went on, successive popes issued increasingly extravagant indulgences every time they ran short of money. In 1391, Pope Boniface IX had appointed men throughout Europe to sell indulgences on his behalf and to send him a share of the proceeds. In 1476, Pope Sextus IV decided that it would be more profitable if indulgences could be sold also for those who were now dead. Hence sons and daughters could buy remission of purgatory for their deceased parents. The whole idea, of course, was totally blasphemous and absolutely opposed to the whole of Christ's teaching. Pope Leo X was simply the latest in a long line of worldly-minded popes abusing their high office for their own benefit.

When Albert and Leo's money-making scheme began in Germany, the populace flocked from miles around to purchase these indulgences. When Martin

Luther heard that Johann Tetzel, a Dominican monk from Leipzig, had been appointed by Albert to sell these indulgences in Saxony, and was hoping to be soon preaching in Wittenberg, he retorted: "Preach in Wittenberg, will he? Then I'll soon knock a hole in his drum!" Martin and his friend Spalatin immediately wrote to Duke Frederick.

The duke refused to allow the indulgence sellers to operate within the boundaries of his principality—the area around Wittenberg. Perhaps Martin and Spalatin—who was Duke Frederick's court chaplain—had persuaded the old ruler that selling indulgences was not biblical. It seems more likely though, that Frederick was more concerned about the loss of the revenue that these indulgences would divert from his own collection of sacred relics!

On the eve of All Saints Day 1516, Martin decided that he would warn his parishioners about the foolishness of indulgences. That day he preached a mild sermon reminding the townspeople that indulgences were useful only in excusing the sinner from punishments imposed by the church; and that true repentance and forgiveness of sins was a different matter.

"The true change of heart that brings true forgiveness and salvation can come only through contemplation of the wounds of Christ, through true remorse, and through the grace that God freely gives to the believer," said Martin.

The parishioners were expecting to gain 127,799 days worth of forgiveness of sins the next day by visiting the relics at Frederick's Castle Church, and they were less than pleased at Martin's sermon. Some of them were particularly annoyed with Martin, since they had crossed the border of Saxony to purchase indulgences from Tetzel in a neighboring village.

"Are you trying to tell me that this indulgence I've bought is worth nothing, then, Mr. Luther?" complained one of the townspeople.

"It's a useful reminder that God is all-powerful and has the right to punish sinful man," Martin explained. "Eternal redemption is the work of our God. A paper pardon is the utmost the pope and all his cardinals can give."

But it was clear that the people wanted something in black and white. Were indulgences "tickets to heaven" or not? Would they really save a man's soul? The answer to both questions was assuredly "no," but Martin had to be sure of his grounds—his scriptural authority—for denouncing indulgences.

During the next year, Martin began working out his reasons for believing indulgences to be contrary to the gospel. He had come up with ninety-five reasons (or "theses") why he believed indulgences to be wrong. But they would have lain unfinished and unpublished if Tetzel's arrival in the vicinity had not triggered Martin into action.

Tetzel was an expert at selling indulgences; he'd been doing the job for twelve years. A few weeks before visiting a town, he would send in a "helper" to publicize his imminent arrival. Then he would come with a caravan of supporters bearing the pope's authorization, displayed on a rich velvet cushion decorated with gold, and chests in which to take away the money.

Tetzel could be sure that a large crowd would be waiting to escort him from the town gates to the main square, where he would preach a "fire and brimstone" sermon about hell, describing in fearful language the terrors to be suffered by the unbeliever.

Next, he would move on to the town's largest church and preach again—this time about purgatory. "Can you hear your dead parents crying out in torment from that dark land beyond hell itself?" Tetzel would cry, playing on the emotions of his congregation. "They are calling out 'Rescue us! Help us out of here! Help us to reach heaven!' "

Tetzel's third sermon was on the delights of heaven. His was a very romanticized view of the place, since Tetzel was trying to present heaven as a beautiful gift that the people could buy for their dead parents. Tetzel recited glibly:

When a coin in the coffer rings,
The soul from purgatory springs.

His other great trick was to claim that all the money collected would go toward the building of St. Peter's Basilica. "That church shall house the bones of the holy apostles, Peter and Paul, those holy bodies that, even now, lie dishonored and abased in the open air . . ." Of course the bodies were not really lying unburied, and half the money was going to pay off the Archbishop of Mainz' debts!

"I would not change my privileges for those of St. Peter himself," bawled Tetzel, like a market stallholder selling cauliflowers. "I have saved more souls by my indulgences than St. Peter ever did by his sermons. There is no sin, however great, that a man can commit for which he cannot be forgiven. Why, if a man were to violate the Blessed Virgin herself, let him but pay his money and he will be forgiven!"

"Disgraceful!" exclaimed Martin when he heard of Tetzel's claims. "How can the man bring himself to voice such blasphemy?"

Three times in 1516, Martin had preached against indulgences and, though Duke Frederick was grumbling about the loss of revenue from his collection of relics, Martin continued with his theme through 1517. Though Tetzel had moved away from the area adjacent to Wittenberg in the summer of 1517, Martin's anger remained undiminished. He was particularly vexed when he discovered a handbook written by Albert, the Archbishop of Mainz, that contained sample sermons for indulgence preachers. It became evident that the errors in Tetzel's preaching were condoned by the Archbishop himself.

Eventually Martin completed his Ninety-five Theses—his reasons why he felt indulgences were wrong. He took these to a local printer who ran off several copies.

Then, on October 31, 1517, the anniversary of his All Saints Eve sermon, Martin took a midday stroll down to the Castle Church. The church door served as a noticeboard carrying all sorts of notices. Taking his hammer and nails and a copy of the Ninety-five Theses, Martin set to work. Little did Martin realize how forcefully he was pounding those nails. The reverberation would be felt throughout Europe and would change the course of history.

8

Escape From Augsburg

Pardon me, most reverend Father in Christ, and most illustrious Prince," Martin wrote to Albert, the Archbishop, "if I, who am but the dregs of men, have the rashness to write to your sublime grandeur. The Lord Jesus is my witness, that feeling how small and despicable I am, I have long delayed doing so. May your Highness allow a look to fall on a grain of dust and, in the spirit of episcopal gentleness, graciously receive my request."

If it was not normal for the clergy to write in those terms to their superiors in those days, the Archbishop might have suspected sarcasm on Martin's part.

The purpose of Martin's letter was to complain about Tetzel's teaching—with its claim that repentance was not necessary for forgiveness—and tactfully to point out that the Archbishop was in the wrong. He was allowing the church, and the good name of Christ, to be brought into disrepute. In a postscript, he asked the Archbishop to look over a copy of his Ninety-five Theses, which he had enclosed, so that he might see "on what shaky ground the indulgence promulgations rest."

The Archbishop exploded. "Who does he think he is? I've paid 31,000 ducats to the pope to get where I am now! What's Luther paid for his position? Nothing!"

Archbishop Albert sent a copy of the Ninety-five Theses to the pope with a request that Martin should be forbidden from preaching in public, or from writing on such matters. Tetzel came across a copy of the Ninety-five Theses, and thundered: "I will have Luther burned at the stake and his ashes scattered on the waters!"

Martin's theses were written in Latin, in the formal academic tones of the day, and ended with an invitation, "out of love and zeal for making the truth clear," for the matter to be debated at a set time and place. But no one turned up to debate with Martin.

Martin's attitude was ambivalent. At once fawning and insolent, he was desperately hoping to bring about the decline in indulgences; and yet he was fearful that he would have to be the one to take a stand on the matter.

He was again, as so often before, looking for someone to answer his questions, to put his mind at rest and take care of things so that he could have some peace. But God had selected Martin to be His instrument for the reformation of the church, and peace would be a long time in coming.

Within a few weeks of the publication, the Ninety-five Theses had been translated into German and had been spread far and wide throughout the land. Countless people suddenly had Martin Luther's name on their tongues. To some, he was a heretic; to others, a great prophet in the Old Testament mold.

The Theses opened in measured tones with a definition of the inner, life-long repentance demanded by Christ. Then they marked out the pope's authority (or rather, the lack of it) to remit sins and their penalties. Martin attacked the power of the pope; the validity of indulgences and masses said for the dead; the popo's motives and Tetzel's exaggerated claims, before suggesting a program of instruction for Christians that would teach them how indulgences might be used for profitable instruction.

"Have you heard the story of the man who died and took his indulgence with him?" jested Martin during his sermon at the Castle Church one Sunday, supposing just for a moment that a dead man could take anything out of the world, save his own soul. "The man found himself at the gates of hell and handed in his indulgence to the Devil claiming that it was a ticket to heaven, and he'd been sent to the wrong place! But by that time the heat had melted the pope's seal and burned the paper to a crisp. 'That's no good,' said the Devil, pitching the unfortunate man into the fire, 'That's nothing but a bit of ashes!'"

Even Duke Frederick had to laugh at that. But something else convinced him that Martin was right. He'd had a strange dream: "I dreamed that a monk, the true son of St. Paul, asked my permission to write something on the doors of the Castle Church in Wittenberg. The pen he wrote with was so long that, though many tried to break it, it resisted their efforts and pierced the ears of a lion in Rome, and shook the crown on the pope's head!'' It seemed to him that God was showing him that Martin's actions were right and worthy of his support.

The lion in Rome, Pope Leo, was indignant when news of Martin's actions reached him. He instructed the General of the Augustinian order to contact Martin's immediate superior, Von Staupitz. "Tell him to silence Luther," the pope thundered.

Meanwhile Tetzel continued to sell his indulgences throughout Germany, with the cry:

The coin that tinkles in the bowl,
From purgatory will speed the soul!

It wasn't very good poetry; but it was even worse theology.

"Within three weeks," Tetzel claimed, "I will have that heretic Luther in the fire. Those who criticize my sermons and indulgences will have their heads ripped off and be kicked, bleeding into hell! Heretics will be burned until the smoke billows over the walls," bawled the friar who thought that he knew everything about an angry, avenging God, but who knew nothing of the humble carpenter from Nazareth.

Staupitz, Duke Frederick, Spalatin, and Father Lang—the prior of Martin's old monastery at Erfurt— all urged Martin to tread cautiously and let the matter die down. He had made his point, they felt, and Martin would be well advised to think of his own future, doing nothing to jeopardize his safe career at Wittenberg. His own bishop saw the good sense in the Ninety-five Theses, but was worried for his own job. He procrastinated, neither supporting Martin nor condemning him, hoping that Martin's enthusiasm for the truth would soon pass.

But Martin had unwittingly turned loose a tiger. Across the known world, from Constantinople to Cambridge, his Theses were translated into the local tongues. From Spain to Hungary, cartoonists were using Martin's words to lampoon the pope. It seemed that everyone was behind Martin, applauding him as he took on the great forces of the Vatican.

In Rome, the hammer blows of the Ninety-five Theses were still echoing. The Augustinian order was due to hold a general meeting at Heidelberg (about 270 miles from Wittenberg), in late April 1518. Pope Leo X hoped that at that meeting Martin would finally be silenced.

Martin and his friends left Wittenberg on April 11, arriving safely at Heidelberg two weeks later. The safe arrival surprised many people, for the Dominican friars had warned that Martin would be killed en route. Others believed that Martin would be captured and taken to Rome in chains. (Tetzel, of course, was of the Dominican order. The Dominicans were particularly fond of indulgences, and most of their income came from selling them. Now that income had been dammed to a trickle.)

Duke Frederick had also been worried for Martin's safety on the journey. He had sent a trusted servant as Martin's traveling companion and bodyguard, and given him impeccable credentials to show if he was stopped.

Martin was exhausted after the long journey, traveling nearly twenty miles per day on foot, but he recovered before the business of the meeting got under way. "I am properly contrite for going on foot," Martin wrote back to Wittenberg. "Since my contrition is perfect, full penance has been done, and no indulgence is needed!" he added, in theological jest.

Far from being in disgrace, as he had feared, Martin was treated as an honored guest. True, he was stripped of his office as district vicar, but that role had been arduous to Martin for some time. He was delighted to see the office given instead to his old friend Father Lang. It was a wise, tactical move on the part of the order. It would mean less traveling for Martin, and hence a reduction in the risk of a kidnap attempt by the Dominicans.

Staupitz spoke candidly with Martin during the course of the meeting: "Caution, Brother Martin. Do not bring our ancient Augustinian order into disrepute."

"If my act did not agree with God's will," Martin replied, "then it will soon fizzle out. But if it really was in His name, let Him worry about the outcome."

The general meeting itself was unexciting. The Augustinians listened patiently to Martin's speaking about his work at the University of Wittenberg. Martin was made chairman for the theological disputations, or debates, which formed the main part of the meeting. The outcry against indulgences was forgotten for a while, and Martin made many friends among the younger members of the order, though the older monks were more cautious.

Luther returned to Wittenberg in a happy mood, satisfied that he was not alone in his fight. His fellow Augustinians offered him a wagon ride, which he gladly accepted. "I went on foot, but came back on a wagon," he later wrote, in words worthy of a conquering general. It was symbolic of the way that his ideas were picking up momentum.

By the time word reached Pope Leo that Martin had not been reprimanded at Heidelberg, the pope was no longer unduly worried. "Never mind. He is only a drunken German," said the pope about Martin. "He will feel better when he sobers up."

But if Leo thought Martin would now be forgotten by history, and would remain an obscure theologian in a far-off land, then he was mistaken. Martin's next writings were the Resolutions—a long and detailed commentary and exposition on his Ninety-five Theses. He submitted these to his bishop, asking him to take pen in hand and strike through anything amiss; but his bishop was staying out of the argument.

Martin sent a copy of the Resolutions to Staupitz to be forwarded to the pope. In a cover letter, he wrote: "The commands of God are softened when we perceive that they are to be read—not in books only—but in the wounds of the sweet Savior," which very neatly summed up the position that Martin had reached by that point in his life.

"I own but one thing," commented Martin, "my own unworthy body, fatigued by constant discomforts. If they choose to take it by force or by cunning, they will but make me poorer by one or two hours of life. The sweet Redeemer, my Lord Jesus Christ, is enough for me, to whom I shall sing so long as I live. And if anyone be unwilling to sing with me, then what is that to me?"

When Martin's Resolutions were forwarded to Leo in May 1518, they went with a cover letter that had been "censored" both by Martin's superior Von Staupitz, and his good friend Spalatin. "I fling myself at your feet," said the final letter, "Revive me, kill me, call upon me, approve of me, disapprove of me, whatever pleases you. I shall still acknowledge your voice as the voice of Christ, speaking through you. May He hold you ever in His keeping."

Pope Leo X needed the sentiment. He was hardly enjoying a period of great popularity. He had just survived an attempt on his life—from within the Vatican itself. Several cardinals were implicated in the plot. About the last thing he needed was yet another affront from Martin Luther, and—for all its humble words—that was precisely what the Resolutions amounted to.

Instead of humbling himself and apologizing to the Holy Father, Martin's words seemed rather to insist on the rightness of his own views on indulgences. The Dominicans in the papal court continually pointed out to Leo that Martin was not merely trying to reform the church, but that he was actually challenging its leader's authority.

The Dominicans' active involvement in the matter made Leo suspicious. Monks were always attacking each other with the peculiar bitterness that is the property of those who feel that it is their profession to be saintlier than anyone else. "These are only the squabbles of monks," he said, feeling that the whole matter might be only a minor rivalry between the Augustinian order and the Dominicans—or the "watchdogs of the Lord," as a popular joke had it—and that he was being used to further one order over the other.

When Leo passed the Resolutions on to a Dominican scholar named Prierias for his comments, a report was produced in three days which—as was expected—condemned Martin. At the beginning of July, Leo finally took positive action. He sent out a summons ordering Martin to appear in Rome for examination. He was given sixty days in which to make an appearance.

To the Dominicans though, it seemed as though Leo was still acting in a halfhearted, disinterested manner. The watchdogs of the Lord were straining at the leash. They wanted Martin's blood, at any cost—even if it meant falsifying evidence against him.

On his return from Heidelberg, Martin had preached a sermon on excommunication. He was not, at that time, being threatened with excommunication (being thrown out of the church). He preached on the topic simply because it was another example of corruption in the church. Originally, the practice had been reserved for important enemies of the church. Now excommunications were laid down wholesale on recalcitrant petty princes; on archbishops who neglected to pay for their offices; and—particularly unjustly—on town councils who attempted to tax beer and wine produced and sold at a profit by the monasteries!

If a man was not brought to heel by excommunication, his entire family—or even his whole town—could face excommunication. It had now become a punishment that the pope used to keep Christians submissive. If indulgences could be likened to a carrot that the pope dangled in front of the church as though it were a donkey, then excommunication was the stick to which the carrot was attached.

Martin attacked, on sound biblical grounds, the pope's use of excommunications which, he said, "fly about by the hundreds, like bats." Communion with God depended solely on the individual's faith, Martin preached, and was not dependent on anything external that the pope could take away.

Two Dominicans copied down extracts from Martin's sermon, exaggerated them, and forwarded them to Rome, claiming them to be a true and faithful copy of Martin's sermon. "Abominable spies," Martin called them.

The pope went wild. It seemed as though Martin was trying to deafen him with hammer blows—first the Ninety-five Theses, then the Resolutions, and now this preaching against excommunication. Furthermore, Martin had had the temerity actually to reply to the criticism that Prierias—the Dominican theologian—had leveled against his Resolutions. Prierias might have been an incompetent idiot, but he was the pope's idiot, and Leo would not have Martin toy with him.

On August 23, Leo put his signature to a document that made the earlier one seem mild indeed. Martin was no longer called to defend his claims. He was plainly denounced as a heretic. Leo ordered Cardinal Cajetan, the *papal legate* (or ambassador) to Germany, who was attending a congress in Augsburg, a good distance from Wittenburg, to arrest Martin Luther.

"When you have him in your power, keep him under a safe guard," said Leo; and he sent similar instructions to Duke Frederick.

The duke felt that for the pope to call Martin an out-and-out heretic was a grave insult both to Martin and to himself for having appointed Martin as a professor at the university. Pope Leo had been tactless, Frederick felt; and even if Luther was wrong, he ought at least to be handled civilly. He refused to comply with the pope's request, and advised Martin to remain in Wittenberg. Martin was glad to comply.

Fortunately, Duke Frederick had much more power and influence over the church's leaders than most of the other German princes did. Firstly, because Frederick was one of only seven people with the power to elect the next Holy Roman Emperor—a very important political position. Pope Leo had firm views on who the next emperor should be, but he would need Frederick's help if he were to get his way. Secondly, Leo needed money and men to fight a war against the Turks. Frederick was one of the few princes who were willing to help. He was too useful an ally to risk offending.

Frederick was thus in a position to arrange for Luther—instead of going to Rome, which would have been the equivalent of walking into the lion's den—to appear before Cardinal Cajetan at a German court. The pope reluctantly agreed.

On September 26, 1518, Martin left for Augsburg. He was going to his death, his friends were convinced. They bade him a fond farewell. Staupitz urged him to go into exile: "You have only the cross to expect. Leave Wittenberg while there is time, and come to me, that we might live and die together."

Martin hoped that God would protect him. "Let the Lord's will be done. Even at Augsburg—yes! In the midst of His enemies—Jesus Christ rules," he said with one breath; but with the next, "Now I shall die, and become a disgrace to my parents." Martin's old enemy, doubt, had returned to plague him.

While seeking to rely on God's ultimate protection, Martin was sure to obtain promises of safe conduct from both Duke Frederick and the Holy Roman Emperor. Not content with that, when he arrived in

Augsburg, he would not meet Cardinal Cajetan until he too gave him safe conduct.

During the five days that he spent waiting for his meeting, an Italian diplomat tried to intimidate Martin, putting into words his own doubts and secret fears:

"Do you really think that Duke Frederick will risk his own lands on your account?" he taunted.

"God forbid," Martin replied.

"Oh? Then just where will you look for protection?"

"Under heaven, perhaps," said Martin, toying with the petty official, "or *in* heaven. God stays the waves of the sea upon the shore, and He stays them with sand. My God is big enough to bring these matters to a satisfactory conclusion."

"Recant!" exclaimed Cardinal Cajetan when Martin, lying face down in reverence, finally faced him.

"I am as dust beneath your feet. I will gladly admit my errors and recant them," began Martin, "just as soon as I am shown from Scripture where I have been wrong!"

Martin was courting disaster. This was just what Cajetan was unwilling and unable to do. The Cardinal had been told by the pope to under no circumstances publicly discuss the matter. Martin Luther was to retract his Ninety-five Theses and his Resolutions. Nothing else would do. But Cajetan, as papal legates went, was a man of reasonable understanding and ability. Gradually he allowed Martin to rise to his knees, and then to stand upright before him. Then Cajetan's pride of scholarship got the better of him, and his eloquence carried him away.

Cajetan actually agreed with much of Martin's writing, and Martin won him round on several other points. But, above all, Cajetan was Pope Leo's man. He would not admit the possibility that Martin might be right. Soon, he found himself arguing with Martin over agonizingly subtle points. In the end, he could endure the discussion no longer.

"Get out!" cried Cajetan in exasperation, after three days of arguing. "Either recant, or don't come into my sight again!"

Cajetan tried to persuade Staupitz to make Luther change his mind, but that was something that the old man was neither able nor willing to do. That night, word spread through the city that Cajetan was planning to arrest both Staupitz and Luther. Staupitz shuddered at the prospect. It was clear that Martin's vow of obedience was in conflict with his new theology. In case the conflict should ever restrain Martin from obeying his God-given calling, the old man released Martin from his vows. (Of course, this also allowed Staupitz to wash his hands of his unpredictable pupil.)

Till the end of his days, Martin would need to owe allegiance to no man, but his conscience alone. But it seemed as though Martin's days were numbered. At daybreak, most likely, he would be dragged off to Rome—safe conduct or not—and would probably be burned alive.

Martin stayed on at Augsburg for several more days, pacing the floor and waiting for Cajetan to summon him again; or for the inevitable arrest to take place. But no summons came, and no soldiers came to take him for burning. Perhaps the cardinal was still making plans to have Martin arrested. Luther could only fret and wait. Eventually, his friend insisted that he leave Augsburg before it was too late.

At dead of night, he was awakened. Allowed only enough time to put on his well-worn monk's habit, he was taken through a tiny gate in the city wall, to a waiting horse.

"I don't know how to ride a horse!" Martin exclaimed. But there was no time for argument. It must have been a strange scene—a monk being hoisted up onto a nag he couldn't ride, in the pitch darkness. Without books, spurs, sword, or trousers, Martin rode off into the night, trying his best to steer the beast in the direction of Wittenberg. The pope had lost the best chance he would ever have of capturing his renegade monk.

9

The Leipzig Debate

A h! Come in, Melanchthon," said Martin to the young man standing in his doorway.

"It's good to see you again, Martin," the young scholar said. "I never thought you'd get back alive from Augsburg."

"Neither did I. Do you know, that horse bounced me black and blue!" After Martin had been put on the horse, he'd ridden solidly for eight hours. When he'd finally dismounted, he found that he couldn't walk properly, and he had collapsed.

"You should have thought of that before getting on the nag," laughed Melanchthon. "But I was referring to your escape from Cajetan."

Martin motioned his guest to the most comfortable chair, and went on, "You know, the worst part about being in Augsburg was the uncertainty; not knowing when I would be sent for; and the worry of whether I would have the opportunity for fair debate or if I would be condemned without trial.

"I was so worried on the way there that, by the

time I reached the outskirts, stomach cramps had prostrated me. I had to be taken the last three miles on the back of a cart!"

Martin had been outmaneuvered, browbeaten, and threatened at Augsburg; but now he behaved as a man who had wrestled with death itself, and had lived to tell the tale. His opinion of his adversary was particularly scathing: "Cajetan was no more fit to judge the matter than a donkey is to play the harp!" Martin said, and his quip would soon be circulated in cartoon form—with Pope Leo as the harpist.

"When I stopped at Nuremberg on the way back, I was shown the pope's instructions—canceled, contradicted, then issued again—to have me bound and sent to Rome, while all the time I had supposedly been given a promise of safe conduct! It is difficult to believe that anything so monstrous could have emanated from a sovereign leader like the pope, but it's true. The Holy Father has gone against his word, and he's attempting to have me unjustly imprisoned."

"You've openly opposed the most important representative of the pope's court," said Melanchthon as he was leaving. "There can no longer be any turning back."

As Martin threw himself into his routine round of lecturing, he did so with a heavy heart. It seemed as though he had burned his bridges behind him, and it would only be a matter of time before the bonfire burned for him.

When Frederick received a letter from Cajetan, demanding that Martin be sent to Rome for trial, the old duke was in an invidious position. Should he hand over his most famous and distinguished lecturer; or should he attempt to withstand the pressures that the pope would surely bring to bear?

Duke Frederick asked Martin for a written reply to Cajetan's letter, and Luther excelled himself with yet another pithy, trenchant attack on indulgences. Frederick was probably sick of Martin and his crusade to reform the entire church; but, to his credit, he was a fair and just ruler who would not hand over one of his subjects to the pope without a fair hearing. Though the duke had been careful not to seem to befriend Martin—always dealing with him through Spalatin, the court chaplain, as an intermediary—he did not relish losing his pet theological professor. As Frederick continued to uphold Martin, he did so with the help of the Holy Roman Emperor, Maximilian, who told Frederick to "keep that monk carefully. We might need him some day."

Martin pushed his luck further by writing to the pope in person, asking that a General Council be convened to discuss his case. A General Council, traditionally, was the only body with the power to countermand or overrule the pope. In consequence, popes were always reluctant to call such councils. It was generally not considered permissible to appeal to a General Council without a pope's express permission. Martin had ignored all the niceties of protocol and gone ahead, with all the subtlety of a bull in a china shop. He seemed to be behaving like a man with a death wish. His friends were all very concerned for him. But Martin was clearly the man whom God had picked for the role of the shepherd boy with a sling, and who was to subdue the ugly giant that the church had become.

At the age of thirty-five, Martin's intellect had

been hardened into steel. His mind was constantly searching for new ideas and concepts with which to grapple. The depths to which he had plumbed St. Paul's theology gave him a vast advantage over his opponents. He had become almost a folk hero in the eyes of the people of Wittenberg, who turned up in droves every time he preached at the Castle Church. But it seemed that they would not be hearing their favorite preacher for much longer. Martin had offered to leave Wittenberg to spare his protector, Duke Frederick, any further embarrassment. The duke accepted his offer on November 28, 1518.

Martin decided to hold a farewell meal on December 1. All his friends were there, including Spalatin and Melanchthon. Martin would miss Wittenberg, but most of all he would miss Melanchthon. He had known this small, thin, intelligent young man for less than four months, but already they were like soul mates. Philip Melanchthon had been appointed Professor of Ancient Languages at Wittenberg. He was the nephew of an eminent Hebrew scholar and a formidable theologian in his own right. Martin's was the stronger character, but in some measure each made up for the defects of the other. Theirs was a firm friendship which, though sadly strained at times, would never break.

As Martin was in the process of making his farewells, a message arrived asking him to stay in Wittenberg. Duke Frederick had some matters to discuss with him. It is unfortunate that history has not recorded the reason for Frederick's change of heart; but it has long been a subject of conjecture. Perhaps it was a setback in the war that Leo was fighting with the Turks, making him more dependent on Frederick's good will, that led him to reduce the pressure that he was putting on the old duke. Or perhaps it was the arrival of a messenger hot-foot from the Vatican.

What the pope couldn't obtain by force, he evidently sought to obtain by bribery. He sent a papal chamberlain named Von Miltitz (a poseur and facile liar) to present Frederick with a Golden Rose—the highest accolade that the pope could bestow upon a temporal ruler. Miltitz conveyed the pope's promise of the Rose, but hinted that Frederick would have to arrest Martin Luther and send him to Rome before the actual insignia would be handed over. But Frederick saw through the ruse.

Continuing the game of cat and mouse, Pope Leo next issued a papal bull, a solemn document bearing the pope's seal, which basically agreed with everything that Martin had said in his Ninety-five Theses! "*Of course* indulgences were intended for the remission of penances, and not for the actual forgiveness of sins," said the pope glibly. Perhaps Leo was trying to lull Martin into a false sense of security. Some felt that the pope was trying to silence Martin once and for all; he had gone to the extent of answering a lowly monk in a prestigious and formal manner, and if Martin did not keep quiet now he must be a very troublesome and argumentative fellow indeed.

The bull, which had apparently been drafted by Cajetan, meant the end of Tetzel's career as an indulgence-seller. Hated by the commoners whom he had cajoled out of their hard-earned money, he retired to a monastery in Leipzig. Miltitz castigated him for his extravagant lifestyle. Not only was Tetzel the father of two children born out of wedlock, he was also receiving an income equivalent to ten times that of the Mayor of Leipzig. He had broken his monastic vows, both of poverty and chastity. Within a few months he was dead. He died a broken man who had received a just reward for deceiving the people of Germany and for playing fast and loose with Christian doctrine.

Miltitz met with Martin while in Germany, and told him, "I wouldn't risk taking you out of Germany, even if I had 25,000 soldiers with me." Miltitz had discovered that too many important people were on Martin's side.

But when this representative of the pope returned to his master, he apparently conveyed the impression that Luther was now ready to recant. The pope wrote Martin a personal letter—a very great honor—welcoming him back into the church and even inviting him to Rome to recant, all expenses paid. Doubtlessly Martin would have found a warm reception—and perhaps a warm bonfire—awaiting him. It's unlikely that he would ever have left alive.

On January 12, 1519, the old Emperor Maximilian died. A new emperor had to be chosen in his stead. The emperor's official title was "The Holy Roman Emperor of the German Nation." Emperors had a nasty habit of being dazzled by the "Roman" part of the name. In the past, many had trampled down into Italy with conquering armies to make their title good. Leo found the prospect unnerving, and was adamant that Maximilian's own choice of successor, his grandson Charles I of Spain, should not ascend to the throne. He seemed to Leo to be particularly prone to delusions of grandeur, and the last thing that Leo wanted was a battle on his own doorstep. In his opposition to Charles, the only supporter on whom he could rely was Martin's own patron, Duke Frederick. The pope, then, was more than ever bound to humble himself to the old duke's wishes regarding his professor of theology. This, of course, put Martin in an even stronger position.

There were seven local dignitaries, "electors" as they were called, who each had a vote in the election of the new emperor. The Holy Roman Emperor had once been an extremely important position, but much of the post's authority had now been delegated among the lesser princes and rulers whose kingdoms made up much of Europe. But the emperor was still much more than a figurehead, and a strong leader could still draw Europe together into a strong, united power. Clearly, Pope Leo wanted and needed that to happen. He needed a strong emperor, an emperor who would be loyal to the pope, in order to further his war against the Turks. This was more important to Leo than differences of doctrine (a lamentable position for a Christian leader to take), and Leo was prepared to let bygones be bygones if Duke Frederick would fall in line with the pope's wishes regarding Maximilian's successor.

In an attempt to win him round, Leo promised Frederick the right to appoint a nominee to become a cardinal. Both Martin and his duke wondered whether Leo was offering Martin the chance of a cardinal's hat? Perhaps the pope had decided that Martin was such a strong and forthright communicator that he would be better to have as a friend than as an enemy. One of the best ways to silence a critic is to promote him! If Leo had had his way, then history might have taken a very different course indeed.

But Leo failed to win the day. On June 28, 1519, the seven electors, including Duke Frederick, voted for Charles I* of Spain as the new emperor. In consequence, Leo was obliged to try to win control of Charles. He needed all the allies he could find, and Frederick was still one of the few on whom he relied most of the time. So, for almost a year and a half, Duke Frederick remained the most important prince in eastern Germany—and Frederick was not going to surrender his theology professor.

The year 1519 was uneventful in most other respects. Martin taught and preached as he had always done. He published many devotional studies, and commentaries on the Bible books of Galatians and Psalms, but Miltitz had dissuaded him from publishing anything controversial for the time being.

Professor Andreas Karlstadt, Martin's colleague at the University of Wittenberg, had made no such promise. He was trying, somewhat ineptly, to champion Martin's theological concepts in debate with Johann Eck, a professor at Ingolstadt University. Eck loved to argue. He thought nothing of a long journey across Europe if he caught wind of a good theological fight. Had he entered politics instead of theology, there would have been a good many more wars in the history books!

Eck had once been a good friend of Martin's. The two had lively, intelligent minds, and enjoyed the thrust and parry of intellectual debate. Karlstadt fancied himself as their intellectual equal and, in Luther's enforced silence, took it upon himself to carry on the reform controversies with Eck on Martin's behalf.

---

*Charles I of Spain became Holy Roman Emperor Charles V.

Karlstadt seemed to have been irritated by Martin's prominence in the field of theology, and perhaps thought to upstage his colleague.

Eck and Karlstadt agreed to hold a disputation at the city of Leipzig. Eck was to provide the theses for dispute, and he chose to produce a thinly disguised attack on Martin Luther's writings. Martin went along to Leipzig as a member of Karlstadt's suite—rather like a "second" in a boxing match. Being under a charge of heresy, Martin could not initially get permission to actually take part in the debate.

The Wittenberg "team" made an impressive entry, accompanied by two hundred of their students. But Eck, who had an excellent memory, objected to the books that Karlstadt had brought and to which he was constantly referring for the first few days of the debate.

"The use of reference books is against the rule of the disputation," Eck claimed. And again, "The learned Professor Karlstadt is putting the audience to sleep with his incessant quoting!" Eck was right, and he carried his point.

Without his books to refer to, Karlstadt was slaughtered. His debating was a catastrophe. He had some promising ideas, but was never able to develop them properly. By the end of the fourth day, he had been worn down by Eck's greater staying power and sonorous voice.

Crowds had poured into Leipzig—perhaps secretly hoping that Luther would take part after all. The disputation had originally been scheduled for the university, but the crowds were so large that Duke George—Frederick's brother—threw open the doors of his castle. Between sessions, Eck surrounded himself with a bodyguard of seventy-five red-and-gold-clad soldiers "to protect me from assassination by the Wittenberg students," he claimed. In fact, the students had arrived heavily armed in case they needed to defend Martin from any popish plots.

Eventually, Martin was allowed to participate in the debate. Excitement mounted in the hall as the miner's son from Mansfeld rose to confront Eck. Each stood behind a lectern, facing each other. A piece of embroidery on the front of Martin's lectern showed a portrait of the saint after whom he had been named. On Eck's lectern was depicted St. George, slaying the dragon. Many saw this as an allusion to Martin, whom it seemed might shortly be slain, metaphorically, by Eck's razor-sharp mind.

The battle commenced with Eck, performing like an accomplished actor, trying to win the audience around with his denunciation of Martin's theology. Martin retaliated. During each of Eck's flowery speeches, he produced a bouquet of flowers, much to the amusement of the audience!

"A perfect forest of words and ideas stands at his command," Eck later wrote of Martin's debating prowess. "He is in no sense melancholic or aloof. He is lively and alert, always cheerful and happy no matter how hard his opponents press him."

The debate covered a long series of controversies. The matter of indulgences, of course, was now dead with the publication of the papal bull six months earlier.

The war of words waged for ten days, the two protagonists marshaling their arguments like troops on a battlefield. Much of the argument hinged on whether or not the pope was capable of error (a point of doctrine that would not finally be settled until 350 years later), and whether a General Council comprised of bishops and abbots was indeed of greater authority than the pope.

"Are you saying," queried Eck, "that you believe a General Council is the highest authority in Christendom and is superior to the pope?"

To many listeners, this was strong stuff, but Martin went further still. "Even councils have contradicted each other," he stated. The only "ultimate authority" that he would recognize was the Bible: "The ordinary layman, standing on Scripture, is more trustworthy than either pope or council without it!"

"But who can best interpret Scripture, if not the pope?" asked Eck. With a pope in office whose knowledge of theology was as limited as Leo's, the argument was specious. Indeed, the two debaters were arguing from totally different premises.

Playing his trump card, Eck asked Martin if the position he was advocating was not the same as that held by Johann Hus—a notorious heretic who had been burned at the stake a hundred years earlier.

Martin confessed that he was surprised at how closely Hus's views agreed with his own. He was identifying himself with a theological position that the church had long regarded as proven heresy! The audience stamped their feet in protest, and Duke George jumped up and, with arms akimbo, let out a mighty oath.

10

The Burning of the Bull

*I*t was an excited audience that adjourned from
the memorable session that day. When Duke
George had made his outburst, there were many
who had expected Martin Luther to be seized on the
spot and taken outside to be burned. Why, he'd as
good as admitted that he was a heretic!

That night, the Wittenbergers slept anxiously,
many fearful for their own safety. But in truth there
was little real danger. Martin was still under Duke
Frederick's protection, and the pope was still too cautious to risk offending the old duke. Even Duke
George was not prepared to risk a bloodletting in
Leipzig. Martin had many well-armed supporters in
the city. This was not like the situation that had existed at Augsburg, where Martin had been virtually
friendless. There was no way that he could easily be
kidnapped and quietly disposed of.

The disputations continued for a few more days,
but they were uneventful. Eck had elicited from his
opponent the public admission that he needed to fin-

ish his heresy campaign. Perhaps Eck hoped for a cardinal's hat for his defense of the pope. It is certain that he had little regard for anything other than himself. In all his debating, he was concerned only with winning. Whenever it looked as though he was about to lose a point, he would quickly move on.

The great significance of the Leipzig debate was that neither Martin nor his opponent could really hope to win. They held such different standpoints that it was as though they were playing a game with two sets of rules. Martin and Eck could not agree on what ultimate truth meant. For Eck, it could only be found in the pope's word; but for Luther, ultimate truth resided only in Scripture.

Eck's viewpoint was the standard one of the Roman Catholic Church, while Luther's was the evangelical view—the view that would soon be the major one in Protestantism. Indeed, the Leipzig debate could be regarded as the first great clash of opinion between Protestants and Catholics.

Martin returned to Wittenberg weary and profoundly disappointed. Deep bitterness emanated from him when he spoke about Eck's behavior. "I have experienced hatred before, but never more shameless or impudent," he wrote to Spalatin, for he was convinced that Eck had never sought the truth, but only fame for himself.

As the year wore on, Martin returned again to his teaching and preaching duties. Christmas of 1519 was to be the last peaceful Christmas that Leo and the church would know for many years. As Leo sat in the Sistine Chapel admiring the new tapestries, the design of which he had commissioned from Raphael, he had little thought for the upstart German monk. Around the borders of the tapestries—depicting scenes from the New Testament—were scenes from Leo's own life. One tapestry, showing Elymas being struck blind by the apostle Paul for his attack on the church, might have seemed to Leo to be an ironic comment about Martin Luther. But it was really Leo who was blind—blind and deaf to the events that were transpiring in the world around him, while he hid himself away in Rome.

Early in 1520, Johann Eck arrived in Rome armed with transcripts of Martin's remarks at Leipzig. On February 4, a commission was appointed, under the chairmanship of Cardinal Cajetan, to formally draw up a condemnation of Martin Luther. Cajetan, in all fairness, had realized the seriousness of Martin's challenges. He proposed that the commission bring in ten theologians to thrash out a final solution—either bringing the church into line with Martin's radical theological breakthrough, or excommunicating him as a heretic. If Cajetan had had his way, perhaps the Roman Catholic Church might have been reformed, instead of being splintered by a series of schisms.

But a reformation in Rome would have denied Eck his glory as Luther's denouncer; so the wily professor conspired to have Leo set up a separate commission, headed by Eck himself. Leo turned his back on the matter, to devote more time to admiring his paintings, sculptures, and tapestries, and the performance of a new play by Machiavelli. His greatest anguish was that there would not be any new work forthcoming from his favorite—Raphael. The great artist died in the spring, at the age of thirty-seven, as a result of a sexually transmitted disease that was rife in the pope's court.

Cajetan was irate that Eck had been allowed to interfere. "Who let that beast in here?" he is reported to have said of Eck—a man scarcely more popular than Pope Leo.

By the beginning of May, the Vatican presented the pope with the draft of a papal bull, "against the errors of Martin Luther." The bull began with the words: "Arise, O Lord. A wild boar has invaded thy vineyard." The boar was Martin, and the vineyard was the church. The bull was known by its opening words in the original Latin, *Exsurge Domine*.

While the pope was preparing formally to call upon Martin to change his views, the Wittenberg monk was working on three great reform tracts: *Address to the Christian Nobility*, *The Babylonian Captivity of the Church*, and *Freedom of the Christian*. Beneath these high-sounding titles were three books that consolidated Martin's position and reputation as the spokesman for a new world order. His words bubbled along like a forest brook, rippling with life and joy.

Martin wrote with conviction and assurance. The change that had begun when he made his breakthrough, discovering the authentic gospel in his tower room, was now complete. The terrible God of judgment who would, as the church taught, condemn people to untold millennia of suffering in purgatory, even after they had been forgiven, was not the real God at all. He only appeared to be terrible, Martin had long since realized, and He appeared that way only to those who could not recognize, in their sinful condition, that they were not ready to accept Him in love.

Martin told everyone who would listen that Jesus

Christ came into the world to reveal to all that God's heart is full of pure, unbounded love. The gospel that Martin had rediscovered beneath the overlay of tradition, contained the whole meaning of Christianity. It was nothing other than the announcement that God is love, love disclosed in the whole life of Jesus, especially in His willingness to die so that people might see how far love will go to help those who desperately need to know its meaning.

Along with that discovery, Martin had made another. It was the realization that Jesus did almost everything necessary to reconcile God with each individual, when He died upon the cross. The only thing that an individual needed to do in order to ensure personal salvation, was to accept (through faith) that Christ's death had made him "right with God." That was something that could never be achieved through good works alone. Theologically, Martin had discovered that man could not be justified, or made right, by good deeds. Justification could come through faith alone.

Good works were but a natural consequence of faith. It was inconceivable that a Christian could willingly and habitually perform actions that were contrary to the nature of Christ, Martin realized. "My fingers are a part of my body, though I did not do anything to join them there," Martin reasoned, "and, though I might accidentally injure them it is unthinkable that I would deliberately take a hammer and smash them. So it is with sin and the Christian. For a believer to go about dishonoring God through lies and blasphemy, murder and fornication, envy and theft is to damage the body of Christ to which he is attached, just as surely as a hammer blow would damage his own fingers."

"God loves sinners," Martin preached. "The love of God does not seek its own good, but it flows out and bestows good on His children. Sinners are not attractive people who are loved by God; they are loved by God and then they are attractive."

Martin believed, with St. Paul, that "nothing can separate me from the love of God that is mine in Christ Jesus" (Romans 8:39). His discovery of the authentic gospel, coupled with the understanding of how it works in humans (justifying them, by grace, through faith alone), had been Martin's epoch-making breakthrough, and the source of his friction with the established church hierarchy.

The pope and his senior church officials could not take Luther seriously because, in their world, the people one took seriously had rank, reputation, and power. They moved serenely through life with the ease of those who could afford retainers to smooth their way before them. To them, Martin was a nobody; and how could a nobody possibly say anything of any importance to them? They had been seduced by the pleasures of the world, and could never know for themselves the wonderful love of God. Their wealth, power, and success depended upon a widely-accepted (but totally false) view that the pope alone held the keys to the kingdom of heaven. Instead of following in Christ's footsteps and preaching the good news to the poor and needy, they had sided with Christ's enemies. They kept the poor in ignorance while they exploited them.

Even many of the people who supported Martin in his reforms did so for the wrong motives. Great scholars such as Erasmus in Switzerland refused to accept the spiritual and theological nature of Martin's proposed reforms. Instead of returning the church to its biblical foundations, many men were seemingly intent on destroying the church altogether, and replacing it with some form of socialism. Martin saw these men as the forces of anarchy, whose liberalism would be disastrous for society as well as for Christianity.

In the second half of 1520, the pope's bull *Exsurge Domine*, formally calling on Martin to recant, began to be published throughout Germany. Johann Eck was appointed to the task of publishing the bull—to pin up copies in public places and to arrange for the burning of Martin's books throughout Saxony, the province of Duke Frederick. He received a rude shock when only three towns allowed him to publish there. Even in Leipzig, the scene of his debate with Luther, the university refused to allow the bull to be published. This was with just cause. The bull had been haphazardly thrown together, listing forty-one supposed heresies, many of which were clearly harmless, taken out of context, or unintelligible. Eck's life was made a misery by the students with their rough humor. He eventually had to take refuge in a monastery for peace and protection.

Aleander, the pope's librarian, had been assigned the task of publicizing the bull in the west of Germany. He generally fared better than Eck, and managed to arrange for the burning of Luther's books in several places. But in Cologne the local ruler refused even to see Aleander, who suffered the indignity of having to buttonhole him while at church. Eventually, Aleander won the chance to have a book-burning at Cologne, though all the pomp was taken from the occasion when the local dignitaries refused to attend. A group of students turned the whole event into a farce when they handed over to the hangman to consign to the flames, not the works of Luther, but old scholastic tomes and ancient collections of dry sermons. On another occasion, a grave digger was given the task of burning Martin's works; but again the irreverent students stole the show by giving the illiterate peasant a pile of anti-Lutheran tracts to burn instead!

On October 10, Martin first set eyes on the papal bull for himself. He had just two months in which to recant, or the pope would excommunicate him. Martin Luther had only until December 10 before the pope would—in theory—lock the gates of heaven itself against him and condemn him to the fires of hell. But Martin knew that those keys resided, not with the pope, but with his Savior Jesus Christ. Christ had died that Martin might win heaven. No power on earth could break the bond between him and his God. God had called Martin, and justified him. The Wittenberg professor knew, with unerring confidence now, that he was obeying God's will and following in the footsteps of Christ. Nothing—least of all the pope's rantings—would make him turn from his course by one inch.

So it was that on December 10, the final day left to Martin to recant and for his friends to renounce him and burn his books if they were not themselves to be implicated and fall under the wrath of Rome, a notice appeared on the Wittenberg Church door where, three years earlier, the Ninety-five Theses had hung. The notice invited "all friends of the truth" to come and help to burn some "godless books" on a small bonfire near the Elster Gate at Wittenberg.

Had Martin's friends rejected him? No, for it was Martin himself who had put the notice there. The books he had in mind for burning were the "godless books of papal law and scholastic theology!"

Crowds of enthusiastic students thronged to the bonfire, while the academic dignitaries came sedately. One professor lit the kindling with a taper, and soon the blaze was roaring, hungry for books. Martin had particularly wanted a copy of a book by Thomas Aquinas (a scholar whose work was greatly admired by Cardinal Cajetan) to consign to the flames. But no one could be found who was willing to sacrifice a copy. Aquinas might be godless, but his books were expensive!

"How about this one instead?" suggested Melanchthon, and held up a copy of *Chrysopassus* by Dr. Johann Eck.

"That should burn nicely," Martin agreed, and soon several volumes of papal decrees and a copy of canon law had joined it on the blaze. As the canon law curled and smoked, the air was sharp and the flames spread a comforting glow to the morning air.

Barely noticed by the others present, Martin stepped forward and took from his monk's habit his personal copy of the pope's bull—the threat of excommunication that hung over him. It was a venerable document. A papal bull was something to be treated with great respect.

"May the fire destroy you, because you have obscured God's truth," said Martin staring thoughtfully at the bull. "Because you have twisted God's Word, may this fire twist you forever."

Then, without hesitation, and without drama, Martin Luther dropped the papal bull into the fire.

11

Diet of Worms

I am deeply ashamed," said Martin to his students the next day. No, his shame was not because of his burning of the bull, but for the antics of the students afterward.

"Was it not enough for you that we burned the godless books, and sang a hymn to frighten the Devil? Was it really necessary for you all to bring shame on this university by marching through the streets of Wittenberg singing and shouting?"

After the professors had left the bonfire, the students had turned the affair into a carnival. One student had carried an indulgence through the streets on the end of a sword. Another, riding on a farm wagon, had waved a copy of the bull, six-feet-long, in the air like a banner. Several had paraded through the streets singing a Hebrew funeral song, directed at the pope.

"Did you have to add banners and indulgences to the bonfire to keep the blaze roaring throughout the night? Why, even Tetzel would have been envious of your pompous parades! This is a serious matter. I will not have you trivialize it with your raucous antics."

The students were shocked. They had often received the rough edge of his tongue, but their professor had never spoken to them quite like this before. This was no academic dressing-down in the usual scholarly Latin of his lectures. It was a coarse, stinging assault in Martin's strong and often vulgar native German.

"These perilous days are no time for silly student pranks and stupid behavior," he told them. "If you really support me then you had better be prepared to face death with me. Our warfare is not with flesh and blood, but with spiritual wickedness in high places." Martin was convinced that the Devil was behind the pope's actions. For a time, he even thought that the Devil was in possession of Leo—that the pope was the Antichrist about whom Jesus had warned His followers.

Martin's anger with his students did not last. How could it, when he felt happier at his burning the papal bull than he had ever felt about any action in his entire life? It was a small thing, but it had captured the public's imagination. The news spread across Europe and soon the world's major cities were buzzing with excitement. No one had ever before dared to publicly burn a papal bull.

By his actions, Martin had put himself outside the church, even before Pope Leo's *Decet Romanum*—the formal bull of excommunication—was issued. Had excommunication occurred earlier, say after the posting of the Ninety-five Theses or the confrontation with Cajetan, then Martin might have found himself to be a friendless outlaw. But now he had millions of supporters all across Europe. People were rallying behind his words like an army behind their general. Change was in the air, and the population looked to Martin as the prophet of a new age. If Martin's new epoch could be said to have begun on one particular day, that day would be December 10, 1520, when the Wittenberg professor divorced himself from the pope's church.

On January 3, 1521, Leo signed the final bull excommunicating Luther. It denounced Martin and his supporters as unbelieving heathens. But the bull would have no effect so long as it remained a spiritual judgment only, and not a political one. To secure Martin's final downfall, Leo wrote to Charles V, the newly crowned Holy Roman Emperor, requesting that Martin be declared an outlaw whom any citizen could kill without fear of punishment. Emperor Charles was then only a young man of twenty. He was ill-at-ease in public, but he was honest and upright. He would not let the pope have his way, unless he felt the request was a just one. The only way to decide was to have Martin's case formally discussed.

Pope Leo was horrified to learn that Charles had called a diet, or congress, at the German city of Worms for late January 1521, which Martin had been invited to attend. Charles was not dependent on the pope, so Leo could not be assured of getting his own way.

The pope's emissary, Aleander, who had helped to publish the bull against Martin, had the emperor's ear and tried to persuade him to send Martin to Rome without trial: "Surely this is a spiritual matter, and not a secular one. The only competent judge can be the pope."

By the time the Diet of Worms actually met, Charles had decided not to invite Martin; but neither would he send Martin to Rome. Duke Frederick who, as one of the seven electors, was present at the diet, was pleased. He had already insisted that if Martin was to be summoned to attend, it should only be under a guarantee of safe conduct from the emperor himself.

Once the diet began, Aleander petitioned the emperor and his electors for nine hours, pleading that Martin be condemned without trial, and without being invited to the diet. Open violence broke out at this suggestion, and two of the electors had to be separated by the intervention of a cardinal.

Uneasy lay the head that wore the crown. Charles had first decided that Martin would attend, then that he would not. Now he was being forced to return to his original decision. One of Charles's first acts as emperor had been to sign a declaration that no subject of the emperor could be tried outside his jurisdiction, nor be outlawed without a fair and open trial. Charles's hands were tied. The only course open to him was to summon Martin to appear before the diet.

In an earlier letter to the emperor, Martin had written: "For three years I have vainly sought peace. I have no desire to be defended if I am proved impious or heretical. But one thing I request, neither truth nor error should be condemned without a hearing." There could be no doubt that the monk was ready and willing to attend the diet.

"Our noble, honored, and esteemed Martin Luther," began the invitation—much to Aleander's disgust.

"That's no way to address a heretic!" he protested, but the emperor and his electors were adamant.

"I must take care," Martin wrote to Frederick when he heard of his summons, "that the gospel is not brought into contempt by our fear to attest to it and seal our teaching with our blood."

It was Easter when the summons arrived. Martin had preaching commitments in Wittenberg, and the imperial messenger had to wait eight days before the monk was ready to leave. When Martin eventually left for Worms, he wondered whether he would ever see Wittenberg again; but he wasn't daunted.

"Goodbye, Melanchthon, dear friend. Though they kindle a fire all the way from Wittenberg to Worms, the flames of which reach up to heaven itself, I would walk through it in the name of God! My hour is at hand; now, on to Worms!"

The city of Wittenberg provided a two-wheeled cart for Martin and his three companions. They did not want their most famous citizen to have to walk. Like a triumphal procession, the small party set off. The emperor's herald, with a huge eagle embroidered on his cloak, rode at the front. He was amazed that people cheered Martin in every village through which they passed. At Leipzig, the city fathers gave him a cask of wine—a gesture reserved only for very important people. At Gotha and Eisenach, Martin was prevailed upon to preach a sermon. But, as the procession neared Worms, his reception began to appear colder. "Go back," Duke Frederick's chaplain sent word to him at Erfurt. "The duke no longer trusts the emperor's promise of safe conduct. Proceed only at your own risk."

Placards began to appear along the route—positioned by the pope's agents—saying that Martin was going to Worms only to recant. Thirty miles from Worms, a count offered him protection in his castle. "Don't go on to Worms; you go to your death! By all means come to my castle. Take refuge and carry on the debate by letter."

"My cause is commended to the Lord," replied Martin confidently. "Surely He who preserved the three young men in the fiery furnace in Babylon still lives and reigns. I shall go on even if there are as many devils in Worms as there are tiles on the roofs! Unless I am held back by force, I will enter Worms under the banner of Christ against the gates of hell!"

On the morning of April 16, a watchman on the cathedral tower at Worms saw Martin's party approaching, and he announced their arrival with a trumpet blast. A hundred horsemen rode out to escort the travelers into the city. Like a triumphant general, Martin Luther rode along the city streets. Two thousand cheering citizens urged him on, while several priests superstitiously touched his clothing. Two dozen eminent townspeople invited him to dine with them. The pope's representative was absolutely furious!

In spite of attempts to have all Martin's writings burned, the monk's books were on open sale throughout the town. His name was on everyone's lips. He had come to offer the emperor 100,000 soldiers with which to ride down into Italy and overthrow the pope, said one rumor. No, the emperor was going to deliver him into the pope's power, said another.

The city of Worms was seething with visitors. There was little accommodation available for so many distinguished guests. It was not uncommon for six or seven people to sleep in one bed. Why, even the emperor himself had to share a room with his chief advisor. Martin found himself provided with accommodations in a hospice of the Knights Templar, close to Duke Frederick's own residence, for security reasons.

All manner of cartoons and pamphlets were in circulation in the city—mainly in support of Martin—and all manner of pleasure was available to the dignitaries attending the diet. Drinking, racing, gambling, eating, jousting, whoring, wrestling, and talking occupied the days and nights.

In the diet itself, the English ambassador sat awaiting an opportune moment to offer the young bachelor emperor an arranged marriage with a member of the English royal family. The French ambassador carried a declaration of war among his papers. Pope Leo's representative had a bull of excommunication to which the name of Hutten—the champion of German nationalism—had been added to Luther's, but he wasn't about to produce it with so many patriotic Germans around.

Language was another difficulty. The various nationalities were unable to understand one another, and the German emperor spoke only French and Latin. This was the bizarre situation into which Martin Luther stepped the next day. He'd spent the morning giving communion to a sick nobleman—performing the duties of an ordinary parish priest. Then, at four in the afternoon, the imperial herald called for him to escort him to the diet.

Martin was sneaked in the back way to avoid the crowds. There, amid the silks and satins, the gold chains and ceremonial swords, the assembled authorities awaited the gaunt, scruffy monk. There, under a canopy at the head of the hall, sat the young, bewildered emperor. Charles was sickly and pale-faced. He had spent much of his life in the Netherlands, and his lack of confidence and experience was conspicuous.

The chairman rose to conduct the proceedings. Martin's heart must have nearly stopped when he was told that Johann Eck was to chair the proceedings, but it was a different Johann Eck who held the title of Chancellor of Trier.

"Dr. Luther," began the chancellor, "you are here by invitation of the diet. You have just two questions to answer." He pointed to a pile of books on a table. "Firstly, do you admit to having written these books? Secondly, do you recant what you have said in them?"

So. It's going to be like Augsburg all over again, thought Martin. *No opportunity for debate; no discussion; recant, or else.*

As Martin was about to affirm that these were indeed his books, his lawyer, a Wittenberg professor named Jerome Schurf, insisted that the titles be read. This was done, and Martin admitted that the books were his. Now for the second question.

"Seeing that it is a question that relates to faith and the salvation of souls, in which the Word of God has an interest, I should act imprudently were I to reply inconsiderately," said Martin, in very stilted and formal language. "Therefore I humbly beg Your Imperial Majesty to give me time to think, so that I may answer without violence to the Word of God or danger to my soul."

The emperor and his electors discussed the situation in an antechamber and agreed to Martin's request "on condition that you answer verbally and not in writing."

The following day the sessions had been moved into the great hall, instead of the forecourt, so that Martin's words were to fall on three times as many ears. He had spent many hours consulting his advisors, reading the Scriptures, and praying for God's guidance.

It was six o'clock when Martin was eventually ushered into the hall. His appearance came at the end of a full day's business, and everyone in the room was tired. Two rows of torches lined the walls, sending dancing beams of light over the gold and jewels of the dignitaries. A table once again stood between Martin and the emperor. On it, his books lay as mute symbols of his faith.

Martin began apologetically before his voice began to take on its usual resonance. With total conviction, he delivered his speech in formal Latin:

"These books are all mine, but they are not all the same kind. One kind deals with simple Christian truth about faith and life. Even my enemies do not object to these.

"Another kind complains about the false teachings and evil doings of Rome. They show how the pope and his followers are destroying Germany . . ." That was a claim that clearly met with a good deal of support from the assembled crowd! The emperor broke in to object, but Martin would not be stopped.

"No, I cannot deny these books, because if I did, I would be opening the door to even worse evils for my country."

Coming finally to the third class of books, he said,

"In these, I have attacked certain persons whom I believe to be the enemies of the gospel." Martin was prepared to admit that he might have gotten carried away with the vehemence of his arguments, for which he apologized. "But I cannot take back what I have said in defending God's truth. If I did, then sin and evil would increase their power."

With that, Martin was finished. But what had he really said? What did it mean? The emperor and a few officials discussed his words, and decided that he had not given a clear, unambiguous answer. The chancellor put the crucial question to Martin once more: "I ask you to answer clearly and without double-talk. Do you or do you not recant your books and the errors in them?"

So this was the crunch. The whole weight of the Reformation was pressing down on Martin's shoulders as he rose to reply. In ringing tones, he delivered one of the most famous speeches in history:

"Unless I am shown by the testimony of Scripture and by evidential reasoning—for I do not put faith in the pope or councils alone, because it is established that they have often erred and contradicted themselves—my conscience is captive to the Word of God. *I cannot and will not recant anything, for it is neither safe nor right to act against conscience.*"

As he finished, the background murmur rose. Everyone seemed to be talking at once. Martin turned away and murmured, "Here I stand. God help me. Amen."

His answer had been so defiant and touching that everyone was taken aback. As Martin repeated his remarks in plain German, the princes and electors began discussing among themselves how they would proceed. The emperor was tired, thirsty, and hungry; he dismissed the session and rose to leave. The irritated chancellor tried to have the last word, but Martin talked him down as he moved toward the door in a buoyant mood. He was enormously relieved at having given his witness clearly and without hesitation.

"I regret having delayed so long to proceed against this Luther and his false doctrine," the emperor wrote that night. "He is to be taken back, keeping the tenor of his safe conduct," he ruled. So the emperor would keep his word after all! But once Martin reached Wittenberg, the promise of safe conduct would be ended. "I am determined to proceed against him as a notorious heretic," the emperor wrote grimly.

For two days, the diet remained locked in debate on the emperor's words. Finally, a commission of three or four people were appointed to show Martin where his errors lay. But the discussion came to nothing. None of the theologians were able to prove from Scripture that Martin was wrong, and Luther refused to compromise. In the end, an archbishop tried unsuccessfully to bribe him with the promise of a good, rich priory!

Eventually, Martin began his journey back to Wittenberg. With him were Amsdorf, Schurf, and Petzensteiner—the three friends who had accompanied him to Worms—and the imperial herald whose job it was to ensure Martin's safety on behalf of the emperor. Martin wrote a remarkably polite letter to the emperor, and insisted that the herald take it back to Worms immediately.

Unprotected, the four companions traveled on to Wittenberg, wondering whether Martin would return to a hero's welcome, or whether another bonfire would be burning near the Elster Gate—this time not for the burning of books, but for Martin himself. He'd made many allies at the diet, but many enemies too.

The party was warmly received at the towns through which they passed; particularly at Eisenach, where Martin had lived for three years as a schoolboy. Then, somewhere between Möhra and Erfurt, deep in the Thuringian forest and miles from anywhere, they heard the sound of horses' hooves drawing closer.

The riders came closer now, surrounding the wagon on which Martin and his friends were traveling. Were these masked riders under orders from the pope? Was the emperor behind this? But there was no time for answers; the five armed horsemen had sprung their ambush. In a melee of curses and blows, they began their attack.

12

Kidnapped!

D isgraceful!" Amsdorf exclaimed when he reached the next village. "Five masked horsemen ambushed us out in the forest! Of course, I argued vehemently with them, insisting that we traveled under the protection of the emperor himself. 'Which one of you is the monk Luther?' is all they would say. I was terrified, I don't mind telling you. Our friend Petzensteiner managed to get away— he took off into the woods like a scared rabbit. He's run all the way back to Wittenberg by now, I should imagine.

"Dr. Luther said that he was the one for whom they sought, and that the driver and I should be allowed to go. I remonstrated with him, but he insisted that we should do nothing to endanger ourselves in the presence of our armed assailants.

"The poor professor was dragged to the ground and hauled off into the woods. Our driver tried to defend himself and was thrown to the ground likewise. He was so terrified, he nearly died of fright! We thought they'd cut our throats for sure.

"Next thing we saw was good Dr. Luther on horseback, being led off along a side trail, with a cavalry cape thrown over his head so that he couldn't see where he was being taken. His cap had come loose in the scuffle and was left lying in the road. As soon as we'd recovered our wits we came here."

Amsdorf tried to calm the villagers, who were in an uproar all around him. Some were crying out that it was all a popish plot to bring Martin in chains to Rome. Others upbraided the emperor for breaking his word. "Surely the good and kind Dr. Luther is even now as good as dead. They'll burn him at the stake for sure," they said.

Meanwhile, Martin was feeling very sick from being bounced along on horseback. The heavy cloak over his head made it impossible to see where he was going; but it also made him stiflingly hot, claustrophobic, and giddy.

Soon Martin realized that the party was riding around in circles to confuse their trail. It was late at night when the party slowed down, and the monk realized that he was being taken across a clanking drawbridge. Once inside, the cloak was removed and Martin gulped in the sharp night air. He was not surprised to find that he was inside a castle. For a moment he expected to be taken down to some stinking dungeon; but he was treated most politely, and taken up to a well-lit tower room—not unlike the monk's cell with which he had long been familiar. A friendly warder brought him food, which he ate before settling down for the night.

The next morning, Martin threw open the shutters on the windows and gave a laugh as he realized where he was. There, stretched out far below him, was the town of his school days—Eisenach—lying between the folds of the hills. This old castle then, must be the Wartburg—the ancient fortress that dominated the town from its tall pinnacle of rock.

There, Martin could see the gables of the home where he had spent happy days with the Cotta family; and there was the church where he had marveled at a picture of Christ sitting in judgment on the rainbow. Far beyond, Martin could see over the broad domains where hordes were beginning to respond to his call to throw off the chains of the corrupt Roman Catholic Church. But why had he been brought here? And who were his captors? Martin chuckled. He knew the answers to both questions, though the pope and the emperor must be racking their brains for the solution, he thought.

———

"Where's Luther?" Emperor Charles demanded of Duke Frederick—Martin's liege lord. But the wily old duke simply shook his head.

"I'll be completely candid with you," said the duke, "I don't know!" It was an honest denial. Under the imperial edict, Frederick would be committing a crime by harboring Martin any longer. He had therefore obeyed the letter of the law by ordering one of his secretaries to arrange for Martin to be kidnapped and taken into protective custody. Martin had been tipped off in Worms, and that was why he had quickly gotten rid of the imperial herald who had set out with him.

"Don't tell me where he is, though; I want to have a clean conscience when I deny all knowledge of his whereabouts," the duke had instructed.

For several weeks, Martin was not allowed to leave his room. Only when his distinctive monk's tonsure had grown out, and his face was obscured with a heavy beard, was he given the freedom of the castle. Clad in the fine clothing of a great nobleman, he explored the rambling buildings. Rumors had been spread around Eisenach that Junker George, a country squire, was staying at the Wartburg temporarily. The castle governor even taught him to act like a nobleman: to stroke his beard; to walk with a swagger; and to hold his hand on his sword hilt.

One of Martin's first requests in his benign captivity was for writing materials. The scholar felt lost without books, pens, and paper. He'd managed to grab hold of his copies of the Greek and Hebrew Testaments as he was bundled from the wagon during his kidnapping, so he was able to while away his solitude reading the Scriptures that he loved so much. His confinement drove him more strongly than ever into his personal theology, and his rediscovered interpretation of God's Word as a force that could change the world. Enforced retreat strengthened Martin's faith; and the preservation of the reformer strengthened the Reformation that was beginning all across Germany.

With Martin out of the way and presumed dead, the others who had looked to Martin, not only as the leader, but as the one who was to do all the work in reforming the church, all had to stir themselves into action. Dean Karlstadt took it upon himself to preach from Martin's Wittenberg pulpit. He did such a good job of propagating Martin's views—and many of his own—that he too found himself excommunicated by the pope. Melanchthon and Staupitz, too, did much to maintain the momentum for social and religious change, though they acted with more discretion and greater wisdom than Karlstadt.

Melanchthon was the first person to whom Martin wrote from his captivity: "I have had much ado to get this letter off, because of the very real fear that my whereabouts may somehow be let out." In the warm, personal letters that followed, Martin bewailed the state of the church, and wrote in graphic detail about his constipation—caused by lack of exercise!

To Amsdorf he explained what had happened to him since the fateful ambush, and added: "Here I am a man of leisure, like a free man among captives."

Many of his letters bore, instead of his address and the date, the legend "from the Isle of Patmos" (an allusion to St. John's place of exile); "from the wilderness"; "in the land of open skies"; or "in the realm of the birds." The latter descriptions were very appropriate. High above the countryside, Martin often felt that he was living in the clouds. Through the tiny windowpanes he could see rooks in the treetops. The sound of their squabbling and chattering brought back memories of the princes and electors squabbling at Worms.

After several weeks of captivity, the Devil himself often seemed to appear to him in the shape of black bats and owls that screeched eerily round the castle turrets at night. There were times when the faith that he had won seemed very unreal, and dark waves of despair overwhelmed him. "I would rather burn in a raging fire than rot here half-alive," he wrote to his friends as he faced his own personal Gethsemane. Once he felt that the figure of Christ was standing beside him, but he bade the shape begone, believing that God reveals himself through the Bible alone. (Here, for once, he was in error.)

Eventually, Martin was allowed to leave the Wartburg castle to go for walks, though a guard always had to accompany him. Once, the governor of the castle took him hunting, but the bloodsport was little to the monk's taste. Soon he began to give his protectors the slip and would gaily ride off to the monastery in Eisenach to borrow books that he needed; and each time he would send his protectors into a worried frenzy till he returned.

If Martin Luther was not an easy man to confine physically, his agile mind and great thoughts were even less containable. His demand for paper and ink became insatiable. When he heard that the Archbishop of Mainz had had the audacity to announce a new indulgence (he had recently added the bowl in which Pilate washed his hands, and a piece of dirt from which Adam was made, to his collection of relics), Martin wrote him a scathing letter that must have seemed to the Archbishop to have come from the other side of the grave!

Soon, many new writings from Martin emerged in print. Everyone realized then that the reformer was still alive, in hiding. Replies to his critics; expositions on Psalms 67 and 38; a commentary on the *Magnificat*; a translation of a work by Melanchthon; and a volume of sermons were among the writings with which Martin's agile mind was engaged. As each was completed, he would send it off to Spalatin to arrange for printing and publication.

By July 1521, Martin was restless and irritable. The thirty-eight-year-old monk seemed ripe for an emotional crisis. His sexual feelings, which he had repressed for years by throwing himself into his work, began to trouble him. His personal letters still complained bitterly of constipation—so much so that his friends feared he had become a hypochondriac. He fought nightly battles with fears and temptations, telling the Devil—often in quite vulgar terms—what he could go and do with himself.

"Your high opinion of me shames me," he wrote to Melanchthon. "I sit here like a fool and, hardened in leisure, pray little, do not sigh for the church of God, yet burn in a fire of my untamed body. In short, I should be burning in spirit, but I am burning in lust, laziness, leisure, and sleepiness." Solitude was becoming unbearable.

Martin began to feel increasingly alarmed at the news that reached him from the outside world. Gradually his old spirituality returned, and he again felt God's closeness. After Duke Frederick and many of the other dignitaries had left Worms, the emperor had finally pushed through an edict formally making Luther an outlaw. If he was found now, he was sure to be arrested and burned as a heretic.

From Wittenberg came news that Karlstadt had returned from a trip to Copenhagen, where he had gone to help reformers there. He had been worse than useless. He couldn't speak Danish, which hadn't helped matters. Now he was trying to upstage Martin by writing new theses on the subjects of celibacy, and the reform of masses.

The idea of celibacy had long seemed in need of reform to Martin. Many people living in monasteries had long since tired of that way of living, but were being forced to stay there because of their vows. It seemed reasonable that these people should be able to renounce their vows and leave the monastery to take up normal life if they wished. But Martin was worried that instead of allowing monks to marry, Karlstadt would go one step too far and force them to marry.

"Good Lord, will our people at Wittenberg give wives even to the monks? They will not push a wife on me!" Martin wrote. In spite of his own reawakened sexuality, the idea of getting married was revolting to him. He was a monk, a community man, with a vocation.

Martin had thought long and hard about the reform of the mass. For a start, it seemed wrong and unbiblical, when the priests took bread and wine, for the laity to be offered only the bread. He also believed that mass should always be a public celebration; the frequent masses celebrated in the private homes of the rich were not a good thing, he felt. Neither could Martin find any authority in the New Testament for the belief that the bread and the wine were physically transubstantiated, or changed into the literal body and blood of Christ; nor that the priest's role was actually to sacrifice Christ anew to the Father. And masses said for the dead seemed to Martin to be totally blasphemous. *How can they call me a heretic when the Roman Catholic Church is itself in such error,* Martin thought.

Many of the events that were happening in Wittenberg greatly alarmed Luther. On September 22, Melanchthon had celebrated an "evangelical Lord's Supper" in the town—a reform of the mass that followed along the lines of the true biblical pattern. But two months later, thirteen brothers in the Augustinian cloister had decided to renounce their vows and simply walk out—throwing the monastery into disorder. Could this have been triggered by Melanchthon's action?

Martin's views on the authority of Scripture were gaining in popularity throughout Germany and the rest of Europe. Some people, however, were exploiting the attack on the pope's authority, not to establish the supremacy of the Bible as the ultimate authority on matters of doctrine, but to substitute a view that God hands down doctrine by sending the Holy Spirit directly. These *Zwickau* prophets, as they were known, had many true biblical teachings, but they mixed them in with many unorthodox teachings too—teachings that were opposed to the reforms that Martin was trying to bring about. These men had great sanctity, but little judgment.

Early in December, Martin made a quick visit to Wittenberg. With his beard and fine clothing, he was not recognized by many, and he was able to stay with his friend Amsdorf without attracting too much attention.

Martin quickly made life hot for Spalatin. The duke's chaplain had delayed in sending certain of Martin's writings to the printers, because he felt they were too controversial. Martin took him to task, and soon the printing presses were rolling.

"What are these clothes you're wearing?" said Melanchthon, when he saw his great friend for the first time in nearly a year. The two quickly fell to talking about the events that had transpired in Wittenberg during Martin's absence.

"Did you know that old Karlstadt got married?" said Melanchthon. "He's married a fifteen-year-old girl, and is urging all the other clergy to do likewise! In fact, he's gotten so carried away, that he claims it's a sin for a religious man not to be married."

"The fool," said Martin. "While I believe it is right and proper for a priest to be married, it's a different matter entirely for a monk to marry. A monk is a very different calling altogether; one that practically demands chastity."

"But what now, dear Martin? Will you return to Wittenberg for good?"

"Shortly," Martin said thoughtfully. "Our next step must be to change all our church services into the language of the people—German instead of Latin. But it will then become imperative that the common people have a Bible in German, which they can read for themselves and from which they can be taught.

"Dear Melanchthon, I must return to the Wartburg and begin translating the Bible—or at least the New Testament, for a start—into the German tongue."

As the Father of the Reformation rode back the 150 miles to the Wartburg, he was full of apprehension. Yes, the reforms taking place in Europe were eroding away several hundred years of corruption. But Martin recognized the possibility that, in their zeal, the reformers would undo all the good that the gospel had done in the last fifteen centuries.

13

Backlash

*I*n March 1522, Luther left the Wartburg castle and returned to Wittenberg. He believed he would be safe there, and he was anxious about the friction that had arisen in the city because of his friends' reforms.

Martin's return was particularly welcomed by Duke Frederick and the Wittenberg town council. In his zeal for reform, Karlstadt had tried to change the habits of generations overnight. At the end of 1521, he began speaking German for parts of the mass. While this pleased many people by enabling them for the first time to understand what was happening, many others were confused and shocked.

When Karlstadt began to give both bread and wine to his congregation during mass, many thought this to be outrageous. They and their forebears for many generations had been taught that the wine was reserved for the priests only. Though Martin was all for allowing the people to have the wine, he did not feel that people should be forced to have it against their will. His idea was to have two tables—one for bread and one for wine—so that each individual could *choose* to take the wine when he or she was ready, instead of having it forced on them.

Karlstadt was now regularly celebrating mass—or "giving communion" as it would later become called—dressed in his ordinary clothing, instead of the lavish vestments that priests normally wore for the services. And he had begun to tell the congregation to take the bread with their own hands, instead of having the priest place it in their mouths. One of his contemporaries celebrated mass in a funny cap with a peacock feather sticking out of the top! "The dam is broken and I cannot stem the tide," said Spalatin. "What a mess we are in. Everyone is doing something different."

The Wittenberg town council had formally approved of many of the liturgical changes, without realizing what the consequences would be. Prompted by Karlstadt, they even approved of the removal of statues, paintings, banners, and side altars in the Wittenberg Parish Church. These carried the flavor of idolatry, they thought. But Martin felt that the attitude of Karlstadt and the council smacked of intolerance.

The way in which the removal had been carried out had alarmed even the town council. They had expected it to be solemn and orderly. Instead, wholesale removal and destruction had occurred. Many beautiful objects had been wantonly destroyed and the people responsible had acted like a rioting mob.

"Paintings and statues, long beloved by many, have been defaced, broken and carried off with callous violence," lamented Martin in his sermon that Sunday morning.

"I am grieved by the insensitivity behind these actions," he told the townspeople crowded into the church to hear their favorite preacher for the first time in nearly a year.

"I am told that students, in a carnival mood, have been singing secular songs in church," said Martin, in a tone of voice that reminded many of the stern lecture they had received the morning after Martin had burned the papal bull.

"I hope that those responsible for the vandalism in the church," he said, looking around at the interior now almost bare of the beautiful hangings and carvings that had made it a worthy "house of God," are ashamed of themselves.

"I have heard it said that one of my colleagues, not content with celebrating mass in everyday clothing, has made a mockery of his appearance by sporting a frivolous cap with a jaunty feather fluttering from it. I believe that his action was intended to show that the dress of clergy is totally unimportant. He has made an ass of himself; and has brought disrespect upon the church."

Martin concluded his sermon by asking for restraint. He asked the firebrands, in their enthusiasm, to remember the "simple souls."

"I would not have gone as far as you have done, if I had been here. What you did was good, but you have gone too fast. Give people time. It took me three years of constant study, reflection, and discussion to get to where I am now." Many people could not accept too much sudden change.

"There are some who can run, others must walk, and still others can hardly creep. Let us therefore throw ourselves at one another's feet and help each other.

"I will do my part," he told the eager reformers, "but we must first win the hearts of the people; for if you win the heart, you win the whole man." Less than a year after his stand before the emperor at the Diet of Worms, as a prophet of change, he was having to lecture his followers on the need to curb their enthusiasm.

People respected Martin's good sense and commanding authority. Karlstadt and some of the other more extremist reformers left Wittenberg, and order was restored. Somewhat guiltily, the students returned to their books.

In the months that followed, Martin wrote a new form of service—in German—and oversaw the printing of his new translation of the New Testament. It sold in great quantities, not simply because it had been translated by Martin. In its way, it captured and defined the essence of the German language. At last, Germans who could read their own tongue had the sourcebook of Christian faith available to them to read for themselves. Martin began to translate the Old Testament too, though it would not be ready for another twelve years.

Duke Frederick, in accord with the emperor's edict, did not harbor or communicate with Martin. Nevertheless, he did nothing to get Martin out of Wittenberg either! His legal representative, Jerome Schurf, regularly reported to the duke about Martin's activities. Since this was the same Schurf who had stood with Martin at the Diet of Worms, and who had been with him when he was "kidnapped," his reports were inevitably very complimentary:

"Daily, he busies himself exposing the errors into which the false prophets entice us. It is clear that the

Spirit of God is working in him and through him. I am certain that he has returned to Wittenberg at this crucial hour only by the direct intervention of the Almighty."

Martin's old opponent, Pope Leo, was now dead. He had been succeeded by Adrian VI. Adrian was a pious, devoted man, influenced by the Brothers of the Common Life who had so influenced Martin's early life. He had great ambitions to reform the Catholic church, though he was very orthodox in his theology and viewed Martin with the gravest suspicion.

In England, Henry VIII had written a dull anti-Lutheran tract and in return had been awarded by the pope the title of *Fedei Defensor*—or "Defender of the Faith." All subsequent English monarchs have inherited the title, as evidenced by the initials F.D., which can be found on all English coins down to the present day.

The events that were taking place in Wittenberg were being repeated all across Europe. Many of the old nobility and aristocracy, who saw their own power slipping away from them, tried to use Martin's ideas for their own ends. But the Wittenberg professor quickly spoke out against them.

Groups of peasants had taken to wandering around the countryside, plundering the rich and even killing people, in the name of "Christian Freedom." Once again Martin spoke out. He explained that freedom existed only within the boundaries of love. Christians could do as they pleased, but only if their actions and motives were bounded by love for God and for their fellowmen.

Nevertheless, many of the peasants listened to Martin's words only when it suited them. He had tried only to reform the church; but others were jumping on the bandwagon with a view to destroying the church altogether. Many factions were seeking their own ends. This turmoil would eventually lead to the Peasant's Revolt a few years later.

Early in 1523, Martin received a letter from twelve nuns in a convent near Grimma. The nuns sought his aid in escaping from the convent to which they had long since stopped feeling any calling to remain. These nuns were like the monks that had left Wittenberg and other monasteries; many of them young people, who had entered religious orders before reaching their teens and before developing any sense of vocation.

Martin induced a longstanding friend of his, the sixty-year-old Leonard Koppe, who regularly supplied the convent with food, to help smuggle the nuns out. Under cover of darkness, the renegade nuns hid in empty herring barrels and were brought— stinking of fish—to Wittenberg.

"A cartload of vestal virgins arrived this morning," wrote one of Martin's Wittenberg contemporaries!

Now what was Martin to do with them? If they were simply returned to their homes, they were certain to be pursued by their superiors. The only alternative was to find them husbands in Wittenberg. Love seldom entered into marriage in those days. Girls accepted whomever their parents thought suitable to be their husbnads or, in this case, whomever Martin thought suitable.

There was only one girl for whom he couldn't seem to find a husband. Her name was Katherine von Bora, or Katy for short. Though she was sensible and intelligent, she was no beauty, and none of the Wittenberg bachelors had taken to her. Her parents were of lower nobility, and she was very choosy about her suitors. These things were going to make Martin's life difficult, but a solution would soon present itself, he hoped. When it did, it was not at all in the way that Martin had expected.

14

Father of the Reformation

B y the winter of 1523–1524, Martin's status
was very ambiguous. He was still wearing his
Augustinian monk's habit, though he had
long since renounced his vows. In the end, Martin
resolved the ambiguity by hanging up his habit, never
to wear it again. Thereafter he wore ordinary clothing.

Karlstadt, as usual, had gone one step further than
Luther and stepped beyond the bounds of common
sense. He and his wife had moved away from Wittenberg for him to become a priest in a rural parish.
The former dean refused to be paid for his ministry,
preferring instead to work on the land growing his
own crops and earning a living that way. This meant,
of course, that he was far too busy being a very incompetent farmer to look after the spiritual needs of
his parishioners, as he was supposed to do.

It was a hard life for Karlstadt and the other peasants. For the previous two centuries, increasing taxation and the rising costs of clothing and other goods had forced the peasant families, that made up most of Germany, into poverty and squalor. These conditions were causing considerable unrest. In 1502, 1514, and 1515, the peasants had protested by attacking their rulers' castles with whatever weapons they could find. All three uprisings had been put down, but only with great bloodshed.

When the peasants began to hear that Martin had dared to disagree with rulers of both church and state, and had written that the Christian is "a free lord, subject to no one," they looked to him as though he were some kind of savior. Many people began to call themselves "Lutherans" in his honor. In 1525, they decided that the time was right to make another violent attempt to gain a better life; Karlstadt did little to discourage them. Martin was horrified at these events:

"No insurrection is ever right, however just the cause it seeks to promote. It generally harms the innocent rather than the guilty," he said. "I am, and always will be, on the side of those against whom the insurrection is directed, no matter how unjust the cause. Those who read and rightly understand my teaching will not start an insurrection. They have not learned that from me."

Christ's cause was to be furthered by word of mouth alone. And Martin stressed that Christ, not he, was the original source of all that he had rediscovered in the gospel. Martin was particularly against attributing too much to him personally; and as for people calling themselves *Lutherans,* "What is Luther?" he asked. "After all, the teaching is not mine. Neither was I crucified for anyone."

In March 1525, the more moderate peasant leaders put out a pamphlet called *The Twelve Articles*, which told of their complaints against the state authorities. Martin wrote his *Admonition to Peace* in reply.

"It is not my intention to justify or defend the rulers in the intolerable injustices that you have suffered from them," he wrote to the peasants. "If, however, neither side accepts instruction and you start to fight with each other—may God prevent it—I hope that neither side will be called Christian. You are only trying to give your unevangelistic and un-Christian enterprises an evangelical appearance."

How true were Martin's words in the light of all the wars that have been fought in Christ's name! Martin would not stand and allow the Lord's name to be tarnished again. After a trip to Eisleben, he realized that the situation was getting out of hand. Killing and looting was rampant. In Saxony, Duke Frederick was on his deathbed and was blind to the situation around him. Martin penned another brief pamphlet *Against the Robbing and Murdering Mobs of Peasants*. "If I get home, I shall prepare for death with God's help and await my new lords, the murderers and robbers."

But Martin need not have worried. The revolt was quickly put down with a massive slaughter of the peasants by the Saxon princes, urged on by Martin's words. "Let everyone who can smite, slay, and stab, secretly and openly, remembering that nothing can be more poisonous, hurtful, or devilish than a rebel," he said, referring to the upstart peasants. "It is just as when one must kill a mad dog; if you don't strike him, he will strike you and the whole land with you."

Martin had seriously overstated his case, and many peasants soon lost their faith in Luther, though they should have had their faith in Christ—not in Luther—from the beginning. After a great battle at Frankenhausen, the Peasant's Revolt fizzled out.

Had Martin used his immense influence on the side of moderation, he might have enabled the peasants to obtain important liberties. But the peasants had alienated Martin by their liberal abuse of his theology. Had he not intervened on the side of the authorities, the heresies preached in the name of freedom by Karlstadt and his friend Munzer—who had sided with the peasants—might have caused more harm than even the abuses of Rome. He was baffled and amused that the peasants should call him "double-tongued," "Dr. Liar," and "Dr. Pussyfoot." His revolution was meant to be a peaceful theological revolution, not an angry bloodletting.

"He lives quite merrily, to the detriment of his reputation, just when Germany needs his understanding and his energy," lamented Melanchthon. But Martin was unrepentant. He had liberated himself from legalism—from things that were "expected of him"—long ago. His theological breakthroughs had only been possible through such liberation—through seeing through the hollowness of prevailing theology to the truth that lay behind it. He no longer felt that he had to launch himself into a hive of activity. It was sufficient for him to be still and at peace with himself. It was important that he had time for his own relationship with God to grow and to mature. But he had something else on his mind too.

While the revolt had been raging, Martin had

made a visit home to his parents. There he had related the story of the nuns who had been smuggled into Wittenberg, and how he had found husbands for them all except for one. "She said that there were only two men good enough for her; old Amsdorf, or myself!" he laughed.

But what Martin had related as a huge joke, his father took as a realistic proposition. He wanted to see Martin married, to carry on the family name. Martin was skeptical. He was still an outlaw in the eyes of the state, and he expected death at any moment. And yet, by marriage, he could both give Katherine some status and make amends to his father for his abrupt entry into monastic life twenty years earlier.

"Marry, yes. But for heaven's sake, not that one!" urged Melanchthon. He felt that Katy was far too bossy and proud. But Martin's mind was made up. On June 13, 1525, a week after Duke Frederick's death, the couple was quietly married in Wittenberg. A fortnight later, they celebrated with a belated wedding breakfast.

"I have made the angels laugh and the devils weep," he wrote to Spalatin, inviting him to the breakfast. Koppe, the merchant who had aided Katherine's escape, was also invited and urged to "ship us, at my expense, a keg of the best Torgan beer. It must be properly aged, and cold. If it is not good, I will punish you by making you drink it all yourself."

Who should turn up like a bad penny in the middle of the celebration, but old Karlstadt and his wife! Looking miserable and dejected, they had barely escaped with their lives from the violence with which the Peasants' Revolt had been put down. Martin was not one to bear a grudge, and Katherine quickly found the couple a room in the former Augustinian priory, which had become their home.

A year later, Martin and Katherine's first son was born. Obviously bursting with pride, he told his son to kick away in his cradle. "The pope tied me down in diapers too, but I kicked them off." Two more sons and three daughters followed in quick succession.

Martin had begun writing hymns and songs for the lute, to be sung in the new church services that he had devised. In 1524 he had published a selection of them, including the famous hymn "Ein feste Burg ist unser Gott" (A Mighty Fortress Is our God). He had resumed his lectureship at the university and was busily engaged in academic work. Two catechisms and dozens of sermon books poured from his prolific pen. And, all the while, he was working on his translation of the Old Testament. "Oh, what a big job it is to force the Hebrew writers to speak German!" he lamented. "It's just like trying to force a nightingale to give up her beautiful song and imitate the cuckoo's monotone."

As the Reformation raged across Europe, Martin found himself in frequent communication with Erasmus, the famous scholar from Switzerland. The two argued about the idea of free will, and Martin became furious when he thought he detected that Erasmus's writings were full of covert attacks upon the divinity of Christ.

Martin's family life was almost curtailed in 1526, when the Emperor Charles tried to enforce the Edict of Worms, which made Martin an outlaw; but many German princes had sided with Luther, particularly after he had supported them against the peasants. At a new congress at Speyer, it was decided that each

German state could control its religious affairs as it saw fit. Charles again tried to stamp out Martin's teachings in 1529, but the "Lutheran" princes protested. From that time on, they were known as Protestors, or Protestants, which is where the name first came into use.

Martin's rousing hymns, simple songs, and German Bible satisfied the people's needs. More supporters were won to his side every day. As clover draws bees, so Luther drew disciples. The son of a Mansfeld miner had become a popular folk hero across the whole of Europe. Emperor Charles was dismayed by this. It would have to stop, he thought.

Charles ordered all German princes who dissented from the pope to assemble for a diet, or congress, at Augsburg in 1530. The prime business would be to reunite the church. Martin would not be allowed to attend. Instead, he stayed in safety at Coberg Castle, while Melanchthon led the evangelical or "Lutheran" delegation. It was there that Melanchthon produced his most famous work—the *Augsburg Confession*—a definitive statement of Martin's reformation theology.

There was, for the first time, hope of reuniting the church, but after three months of discussion, Emperor Charles lost his patience and ordered the evangelicals to return to the Roman Catholic Church, under threat of death. They refused, but a war with the Turks took Charles away from Augsburg before he could make good his threats. In this way, Melanchthon had been as firm in his stand before Charles at Augsburg as Martin had been before the emperor at the Diet of Worms. There could be no compromise.

In the Netherlands, the first martyrs for Luther's

reformation cause met their deaths. In Zurich, Ulrich Zwingli had led the Swiss church away from Rome. In England, Henry VIII was still a firm supporter of the pope; but, within three years, he would appoint himself leader of the Church of England and break with Rome over the issue of his divorce from Catherine of Aragon and his wish to marry the ill-fated Anne Boleyn.

At the Diet of Speyer, in 1544, an attempt was made to "patch up" the Roman Catholic Church. If the Catholic bishops would concede evangelical theology and fulfill their proper duties, then the Protestants would agree to "return to the fold." But a new pope, Paul III, condemned the diet, and the attempted reunion fell through. In 1545, Pope Paul was forced to call a General Council at Trent. The Protestants were excluded, as the Roman Catholics effectively cut themselves off from the rest of the Church.

While great events were happening in the world, Martin was contented with the more everyday joys of family life.

"Before I married Katy," he said, "my bed was not made for a whole year!"

Katy was good for him. She took in students to help make ends meet; though Martin was so kind toward them that he would not make them leave even when they had no money to contribute to their upkeep. Instead, they would sit at the supper table debating with Martin, and asking him questions about his life. Many of his casual remarks were taken down by the students, and later published in a book called, appropriately, *Table Talk*.

Martin began each day with three hours of private prayer, and then joined the family to say the Creed, the Ten Commandments, the Lord's Prayer, and one of the Psalms. The great scholar remained faithful to his God, even in the face of personal sorrow. Two of his children died young—one of them only a year old—but Martin did not resent God taking them from him. "In spirit I am happy," he said when his beloved Lena died, aged fourteen. "But the flesh sorrows and will not be comforted; the parting grieves me beyond measure. I have sent a saint to heaven."

"What a fine fellow I am," Martin had once said humorously. "For a thousand years there can't have been nobler blood than Luther's. Cardinals, kings, princes, bishops, pundits innumerable, and three popes have striven for the honor of being my hangman!" In the end, it was his own weak body that was to be his downfall.

In November 1545, he gave his last lecture at Wittenberg—on the book of Genesis—and took himself to Mansfeld to help resolve a bitter dispute between two counts, who were brothers. It was hardly a worthy task for the great reformer, and yet he felt a loyalty to his old home town. When he arrived, he found that the brothers had been called to the wars. Martin was obliged to make a second weary journey, in the dead of winter. The dispute was finally settled at Eisleben on the very day that Martin preached his last-ever sermon, which he had to leave unfinished due to his physical frailty and weakness.

"Old, spent, worn, weary, cold, and with only one eye to see," as he described himself at that time, he could do nothing but lie down and die where he was, in the town where he had been born and baptized. In February 1546, on his deathbed, he prayed loudly to God and commended his spirit into His hands. He murmured three times that, "God so loved the world that He gave His only Son, that whosoever believes in Him shall not perish, but have everlasting life"—the words from John's gospel that were the cornerstone of his whole life. Then the great man breathed his last.

When Melanchthon heard of Martin's death, he cried "Alas! The chariot of Israel and the horsemen thereof"—the remark that Elisha had made on the death of Elijah. Stricken and silent, too full of tears for words, he was comforted only by the voice of a girl in the street outside singing one of Martin's greatest hymns:

A mighty fortress is our God,
A trusty shield and weapon.
He helps us free from every need
That hath us now o'ertaken.

More than four centuries later, Martin Luther is still regarded as one of the most truly godly men who ever lived. Many believe he did more to put the Church back on the right path than any other man. More books have been written about him than any other person, with the exception of Christ.

If God could make use of even a small frightened boy, cowering beneath the bedclothes in Mansfeld all those years ago, he can surely use anyone. He could even use *you*.

Acknowledgments

I am indebted to the many authors and Luther
scholars whose work I have consulted in the
course of the preparation of this book. They are,
in alphabetical order: Messrs. Atkinson, Bainton,
Booth, Brosche, Cowie, Crompton, Cubitt, Ehrhardt,
Ellis, Evennett, Fife, Haile, Harris, Heyck, Hoffmann,
Klein, Kleinhans, Kuiper, Lipsky, Lovy, Lunn, Mar-
ius, Mee, Pittenger, Rupp, Saarnivaara, Siggins,
Strohl, Thiel, and Todd.

This book is a young person's guide to Martin
Luther (though I hope it will commend itself to a far
wider readership). I have endeavored, above all, to
make his story readable. Obviously much of the di-
alogue, and even some of the incidents of his early
life, are purely conjectural. But where I refer to something that Luther—or one of his contemporaries—has
written, I am referring to authentic documents. I hope
that the discerning reader will not be affronted by the
way I have dramatized Luther's life; and will excuse
the frequent simplifications that I have made in the
interest of clarity.

Mike Fearon
London